What is Special Education?

John Fish

Open University Press
Milton Keynes • Philadelphia

Open University Press
12 Cofferidge Close
Stony Stratford
Milton Keynes MK11 1BY

and
242 Cherry Street
Philadelphia, PA 19106, USA

First Published 1989

British Library Cataloguing in Publication Data

Fish, John
    What is special education? – (Children
    with special needs).
    1. Special education
    I. Title II. Series
    371.9

ISBN 0-335-09536-4
ISBN 0-335-09535-6 Pbk

Library of Congress Cataloging-in-Publication Data

Fish, John.
    What is special education?/John Fish.
        p. cm. – (Children with special needs series)
    Bibliography: p.
    Includes index.

    ISBN 0-335-09536-4 ISBN 0-335-09535-6 (pbk.)
    1. Special education – Great Britain. I. Title. II. Series.
LC3986.G7F56 1989
371.9 – dc 19   88-39508
                                                                       CIP

Typeset by Colset (Pte) Ltd
Printed in Great Britain by St Edmundsbury Press, Bury St Edmunds

Contents

Series Editors' Introduction

In John Fish's previous book in this series, *Special Education: The Way Ahead*, he emphasised that planning special educational services is an integral part of planning the education service as a whole. Setting out the principles which should determine a rationale for special education, he urged that special educational arrangements be developed on a service-delivery model where the child needs them and not where the professionals prefer to work. He wrote:

> The future development of a rationale for special education should recognise more clearly that the traditional institution as a base for special education is being replaced by a range of arrangements which require a more flexible response from professionals.

What informed and inspired John Fish's concerns then was the belief that society, and the education service in particular, must demonstrate that it is helping to educate potentially contributing citizens who can play a useful part in the communities in which they live; that the handicapped are not a dependent group and objects of charity, but people capable of shouldering responsibilities and with a vital contribution to make.

This book is underpinned by the same belief and takes a cold, hard look at what is special about special education. It analyses what needs to be done if provisions for the handicapped are to be planned as an integral part of education and if they are to deliver a comprehensive and flexible service designed to meet the various and changing needs of all pupils throughout their education. What John Fish proposes is essentially practical. It is also urgently timely. For not only are present provisions demonstrably failing to meet the needs of many of our handicapped pupils, they are often dependent on charity, invariably *ad hoc* and fortuitous; and, today, they are in danger of being further distorted by the simplistic notions of grading children as 'above average, below average or average', and by the woolliness and imprecision which results from inadequately trained and equipped professional personnel. The 1981 Act may well have resulted in a qualitative change in thinking about needs rather than categories and about integration rather than segregation; but, conceived in haste on the cheap, it has resulted in few quantitative or qualitative changes in services to meet ascertained needs or to realise each pupil's potential.

What is Special Education? assesses the present situation squarely and fairly. We would expect nothing less from John Fish, whose whole career has confronted the reality of educational provisions and been inspired by compassion and idealism. This was manifest in his work as HM Staff Inspector for special education in England and as one of the Department of Education and Science's assessors on the Warnock Committee. He was chairman of the Inner London Education Authority's Committee reviewing provision in the metropolis for children with special needs and was involved with the OECD special education project. During 1987/88 he was an Honorary Fellow in the Educational Psychology and Special Educational Needs Department at the London Institute of Education.

What makes this book essential reading is that for the first time the key questions about the nature of the provision of education in special schools, units and classes are asked and answered within the framework of a service-delivery model. The nature and quality of what is provided, the levels of service offered to supplement or replace the normal processes of education and the functions or rôles of a unified support service to schools and colleges are brought into sharp focus. In this context curriculum is given proper attention and the author is at pains to point out that, although the 1981 Act embodied the concept of special educational need as a consequence of a learning difficulty, it is not sufficiently recognised that learning difficulties embrace social, behavioural and emotional difficulties as well as cognitive ones. Unless the education of all children gives adequate attention to these dimensions of development we are in danger of creating more social misfits and disturbed and inadequate people than we have already. Here relativity is an essential concept and assumes improvement in the ability of ordinary schools to deal appropriately with individual differences and needs. Relativity also implies that all elements in a special education system, including special schools themselves, are directing their efforts to improving this capacity in all schools. For, it is argued, the working basis for defining special education is the degree of variation in essential characteristics or dimensions by which ordinary education is modified or supplemented to meet special needs.

Within this conceptual framework John Fish sets out in detail the situations, resources, dimensions and levels of provision and the consequent contributions of professional, non-professionals, agencies and, of course, parents. In much of this he is not simply demonstrating the fine tuning necessary within the educational system: he is providing and defining the language and the criteria we all need if we are to be accountable for the educational progress and for the standards of all our children and young people, with and without special needs alike.

Because of its significance and scope and its logical and closely argued recommendations, *What is Special Education?* is not only a book for planners and administrators, although it is certainly essential reading for them. John Fish conceives this book as a contribution to a necessary dialogue. Because he has so perceptively delineated the territory we must cross, and provided the criteria and terms we shall need as we traverse it, his book is essential reading for all professionals and non-professionals as well as concerned and committed parents who wish to contribute to that dialogue. Thanks to him we will be better able to articulate our concerns and specify the resources of time, technology and expertise we consider essential to plan and provide for realising the potential of pupils with special needs.

Phillip Williams
Peter Young

Preface

The government's proposals to reform the education system and to institute a national curriculum came just as the implementation of the 1981 Education Act was taking effect in many areas. These proposals for change said little about children and young people with special educational needs.

It was difficult to comment on them for a number of reasons. At a superficial level few paragraphs were devoted to the education of children with special educational needs either in consultation documents or the draft Bill. Another major difficulty was the lack of an agreed descriptive system for special education. When asked 'What is special education?' many reply 'That is a good question'; but few answer it.

This book could not have been written without valuable discussions and exchanges with many in the field of special education over a number of years. But two influences must be acknowledged. First, many of the ideas in this book were developed with the help of a group attending the Cambridge Institute of Education Special Education Summer School in 1987.

Second, the privilege of being an Honorary Fellow in the Educational Psychology and Special Educational Needs Department at the London Institute of Education during the academic year 1987/88, provided a further unique opportunity to pursue the question. The support of Klaus Wedell, and other members of staff, and students was invaluable in clarifying ideas.

However, in recording my gratitude for the explicit and implicit help received there is no suggestion that those giving it are in agreement with the approach outlined in this book. It must also be said that acceptance of the ideas in this book is less important than initiating a necessary debate about the nature of special education, how to define it and how to evaluate it in a changing educational system.

CHAPTER 1

Warnock Plus Ten

The Warnock Committee, studying special education, was set up in 1974 and completed its work in 1978. During that period there were three different governments. It was agreed to set up the committee during a Conservative administration. Its members were then appointed and the Committee's report completed during the last Labour administration. Such implementation as has occurred has taken place during what has turned out to be a long period of Conservative administration. Ten years after the publication of the Committee's report *Special Educational Needs*,[1] it is time to take stock. The context in which special educational needs arose and were met at the time the Committee sat has changed. New policies for the education system have been introduced and more radical changes are the subject of legislation.

When the Report was published comprehensive education was an agreed policy and the majority of children of secondary age were attending a neighbourhood school. The relative definitions of need and provision, and the rather tentative move towards integration, which were embodied in the 1981 Education Act [2], reflected a belief that it was right to attempt to provide for all, according to need, within a common secondary school.

Since that time the government has shown an increasing lack of confidence in local education authority primary and secondary schools. Comprehensive schools, in particular, have been under attack for poor standards and an inappropriate curriculum. A 'back to basics' approach has embodied a crude restatement of the traditional and competitive system found wanting in the 1950s.

New legislation has required schools to provide more information to parents and to give them more say in management. Further powers to manage resources, and to opt out of local education authority control, are to be given to school governors in the next few years. These new initiatives are likely to result in a more fragmented pattern of educational provision and an implicit hierarchy of schools, determined by parental choice.

The changes provide a major challenge to those working in special education. A number of key issues have to be reconsidered and policy objectives reformulated. For example, integration may no longer be an issue related solely to being educated in comprehensive primary and secondary schools, but become a much more complex issue of *access* to the same range of schools as other children.

As well as evaluating progress since 1978 it is necessary to establish firm parameters for special education in a changing primary and secondary school context. A close study will show that existing definitions are vague and there are few agreed descriptions of what is delivered in the name of special education. The purpose of this book is to attempt a more precise definition and to open up a debate on the future development of special educational services.

Special Educational Provision

Since the publication of the Warnock Report and the 1981 Education Act considerable attention has been paid to the assessment of children with more complex special educational needs and to procedures for making statements of those needs. Far less attention has been paid to the nature of special education and the means by which it is delivered. This is particularly true about the means of meeting the wider range of needs covered by the Report and the Act for which a statement is unnecessary.

Administrative, professional and academic efforts have been focused on describing special educational needs accurately. Without the reassuring, but inappropriate, use of categories these efforts have resulted in new labels for needs rather than new thinking about how to meet them.

Many factors, not least limited resources, have resulted in provision to meet needs being expressed either in very general terms or in terms of what is available rather than what is needed. Some local education authorities – for example Manchester, Sheffield, Derbyshire and the Inner London Education Authority – have taken the opportunity to carry out a radical review of provision and to replan their special education service. Others have continued to respond to needs in a relatively *ad hoc* way. In general much more must be done to specify with greater precision the forms of special education that it is possible to provide, within existing resource limits, within a unified local authority special education service.

Against the background of a national curriculum framework[3] and of major changes in primary and secondary schooling, it is necessary to look more closely at how a special education service should respond to the needs of individuals in the schools of the future. The following chapters will look at ways of defining different forms of provision more precisely. They will look at how special education teaching time is managed and whether resources can be used more effectively. The question to be attempted is, can a more rational description of what is done in the name of special education facilitate resource allocation and accountability?

Disability and Special Educational Need

It should not be necessary to go over old ground; but memories are short. There is still considerable confusion about definitions of handicap and special educational need. All too often handicaps are attributed to flaws in the individual rather than to the outcomes of interaction with others, to administrative barriers and to public attitudes. The nature of educational and social situations individuals have to face may play an important part in determining the extent to which particular disabilities are handicapping. It is important to recognise that handicaps are relative and situational and that they are defined by administrative criteria and *not* by disabilities.

The Warnock Report states that there is only one population of children, some of whom have disabilities and special educational needs. There are not two populations, the hale and the handicapped, or the ordinary and those with special educational needs. This single population has more common needs than differences. A single population of children with different experiences, with different arrays of abilities and with more or less effective parenting and teaching will give rise to a variety of learning styles, aspirations and achievements.

It is only natural to attribute the poor standards achieved by some children to their inherent deficits rather than to ineffective or inappropriate parenting or teaching. Nevertheless the 1981 Act abolished categories and special educational needs are no longer defined in terms of particular individual deficits: such needs are now defined by a child's response to a particular school in a particular local authority and to the extent of his or her learning difficulties in comparison with others. The Act's definitions clearly imply that the quality of education in general and the situations experienced by different individuals have a central and crucial part to play in the emergence of special educational needs.

The new proposals for benchmarks and for testing individuals at different ages appear to have forgotten the lessons of the 11 + . The achievement of standards, in terms of test scores or criteria, by some children means that others are seen to fail. Indeed the idea that 'statements of special educational need' should be used to absolve children from meeting standards is a regressive step. Not only does it automatically lower expectations for all those who are the subject of statements but it represents a move to recategorise children rather than treat them as individuals. The difficult problem is now to promote and assess improved performance without the disadvantaging discrimination which often results to those unable to meet relatively arbitrary criteria.

It has to be recognised that it is social pressure, administrative necessity and resource allocation which gives rise to labelling individuals as handicapped or as having special educational needs. The educational monograph 'Disability and Restricted Opportunity' published by OECD/CERI[4] discusses the concept of handicap in developed countries. It shows how services have begun to recognise that the handicapping effects of disabilities are individual and may change from situation to situation and from time to time over a lifespan. To have the same disability is not automatically to have the same needs or the same handicaps. Nevertheless, many agencies continue to deliver relatively inflexible packages of benefits and services on an 'all or nothing' basis to those assessed as falling within particular categories.

While it is important not to underestimate the nature and significance of particular disabilities, it is situations, experiences and relationships which determine the degree to which they are handicapping. Similarly, special educational needs which require additional or different provision are relative and determined by the circumstances in which children are being educated. They are relative to the ability and willingness of schools to provide for all the children who attend them.

Definitions, used to describe individuals or their entitlement to services and resources, will be discussed more fully elsewhere. But it needs to be recognised that special education is entering a period of dissonance between the 1981 Act's relative definitions of need and provision, which have gained widespread acceptance, and an apparent intention to define more precisely the standards to be reached by groups of children of a particular age, who may be defined as 'above average'

'average' or 'below average', thus reintroducing categories for the
majority of children if not for those with special educational needs. For
the educationalist the complex issue of norm-referenced and criterion-
referenced assessment underlies much of the debate. But, the public
debate is conducted in relatively simplistic terms with an underlying
belief that a hierarchy of fair and useful performance criteria can be
found to grade children. This presents a profound challenge to the
objective of according equal worth to all children within the education
system, whatever their achievements, together with an equal entitlement
to high quality education.

From Warnock to Legislation

Both a change of government and the need for a more careful use of
resources prolonged the period between the Warnock Report and any
government action. Indeed, it is doubtful if legislation would have come
when it did if it had not been for the International Year of the Disabled
Person in 1981. It could be argued that the search for a relatively low cost
project which could show good intentions ended up with special
educational legislation as one of the least expensive alternatives.
Although it was passed with the proviso of no additional resources,
many considered that once on the statute book, the Act's provisions
would ensure that resources were allocated to its implementation. This is
certainly what has happened in many local authority areas. It is less
evident that the government has shown any enthusiasm for an
enlightened Act which is seen as among the most progressive in an international context.

The 1981 Act embodied the concept of special educational need as a
consequence of a learning difficulty. What is still not widely understood
is that the term learning difficulty was used in the psychological sense in
which all behaviour is learned. Thus emotional, behavioural and social
difficulties are embraced as well as the more traditional cognitive ones.
The Act was significant in defining needs and provision individually and
clearly making primary and secondary schools responsible for finding
and meeting special educational needs.

The Act was notable for the attention given to assessment and parental
involvement, particularly where the local authority was to make a
statement of needs and provision with which it had to comply. It also
made rather tentative steps towards an integration policy by reversing
the approach of the 1944 Act, which was to look for provision first within
special schools. The 1981 Act said that authorities should look first at
possible provision in primary and secondary schools but hedged this

statement with so many qualifications that only the most committed and determined were likely to look very hard for integrative arrangements.

The 1981 Act did not include further education. Its provisions cover individuals up to the age of 18 + if they remain in school but do not do so if the individual chooses to attend a college of further education after the age of sixteen.

The Department of Education and Science issued two Circulars after the Act was passed.[5, 6] The first was explanatory and the second indicated the way changes should be made. The second took so long to issue that it did not come out until January 1983 and local education authorities were expected to implement the Act on 1 April the same year: just three months to institute one of the most significant series of changes in the field for nearly 20 years! Since the beginning of 1983 the Department has been silent. It awaited research results, now available, concentrated on gathering information about the number of children for whom statements had been made. It appeared singularly indifferent to the wider implications of the Act, monitoring neither the general extent of special educational needs for which a statement was not considered necessary nor the kinds of provision being made for children with that degree of need.

Developments to Date

There have been a number of Department-sponsored initiatives in the years since the Warnock Report and the Act. Among these are teacher training initiatives, micro-electronic programmes and some early childhood initiatives. Many of these followed the introduction of education support grants – a new power acquired in the 1980s – to centrally fund developments considered to have priority by the Department of Education and Science. The other major development was the significant increase in provision for students with special educational needs within further education colleges. The work of the Further Education Unit and development of the staff training programme *From Coping to Confidence*,[7] designed for college based in-service training, made important contributions.

The funding of one-term courses made a substantial contribution to the preparation of teachers in primary and secondary schools to detect and meet special educational needs. More teachers were helped to develop the skills necessary to take responsibility for giving a lead in primary and secondary schools. Training institutions and the special education field had much to offer as to the most helpful learning conditions for the children concerned, the assessment of children and the devising of individual programmes. What was less certain was what forms of special educational teaching arrangement which might make the most effective use of the available time. As subsequent chapters will argue, a major weakness in the training programmes was the lack of adequate tools to describe and cost what might be done and a lack of general agreement about what, in practice, constitutes special educational provision for the wider range of needs.

The micro-electronics programme, based around four regional resource centres with training courses for users, has improved the level of available experience and competence in this aspect of special education. The influence of new technology on where and how special education may be provided in the future remains to be considered. At present the main effects of the initiatives have been to improve what is done where it has always been done.

The provision of appropriate services and facilities for children with special educational need under the age of five was one of the Warnock Report's three priority areas. Only a few education authorities have had substantial nursery school and class provision within which to address this priority. For the majority a resource-starved amalgam of play groups, social service nurseries and under-five provision in schools has been all that has been available. Such places as exist are taken up by children of effective parents and of social priority families. There has, however, been some central funding for Portage-type home teaching programmes. Their value is established though their availability is patchy; but the continued funding of some programmes may be uncertain.

Two other major influences have been evident. The first of these has been the dialogue with parents, professionals and administrators arising within the three research projects, funded by the Department, carried out by the London University Institute of Education, Manchester University and the National Foundation for Educational Research.[8, 9, 10, 11] Their existence and interactive mode of work stimulated discussion. The second was the publication by the Inner London Education Authority of its review *Educational Opportunities for All?*[12] This review of provision in a major city emphasised the need to develop a coherent special education service out of the many *ad hoc* initiatives which had been taken in recent years.

The longer-term impacts of these influences in a period of major change in the education system is uncertain. It is evident that progress has been made but that much of it has been in separate, unrelated programmes. On the positive side there has been a recognition of the special educational implications of all programmes. On the negative side this recognition seldom occurs until after the main thrust of the programme has been agreed.

What is Special Education?

The past ten years have seen much greater precision in the way programmes for individual children with special educational needs have been written. A similar increase in precision has been evident in the curriculum statements of many special schools. However, most current special education service definitions of objectives and patterns of work are woolly and/or warm-hearted general statements of intent. Many submissions for resources still rely on stimulating a charitable attitude to helping 'the handicapped'. There is seldom a precise statement of what is going to be done, how long it will take and what criteria will be used to know whether it has been done.

It is often argued that a lack of resources is the main reason for vagueness and imprecision. Later chapters will imply that the personnel in the special education field do not have the tools, the training and the experience to make more precise formulations. It will further be argued that only a more precise definition of the levels of intervention provided by a special education service and more precise job descriptions for individuals will protect resources and make a reasonable case for appropriate special educational provision in a changing school system where 'economic' considerations may be paramount.

The Development of Provision

Since the Warnock Report and the 1981 Act the provision of special education has been marked by expediency rather than policy. For administrators under parental pressure placement – *where* children are to receive special education – has commonly taken precedence over *what* they are to receive; a hierarchy strongly influenced by parental attitudes to integrative arrangements. Another example is the appointment of part-time teachers and non-teaching assistants, without special education training or experience, to support individuals who are the subject of statements in primary and secondary schools. Extra teaching and non-teaching hours of any kind have thus been equated with special education.

The kinds of programme or regime that special schools and units can provide have not been specified by local education authorities. Such schools and units have been expected to provide precisely what the children admitted to them need. Entrepreneurial management or inertia have compounded the difficulties so that schools and units have been stretched to accommodate more varied individual needs than they can or should meet. Another form of provision which has increased in scale is advisory and support teaching work. A change in the working patterns of 'remedial services' and a recognition that primary and secondary schools need support teaching services has become evident.

Describing Special Educational Provision

Whether we turn to national guidelines, academic research or local policies there is a dearth of accurate description of what is going on during the time a child is said to be being 'specially educated'. A number of questions have to be asked about the nature of provision in special schools, units and classes. They include:

- What is actually being done in a setting described as providing 'special education'?
- What are the variables, for example curriculum, relationships and techniques, which determine the nature of those settings?
- What are the limits of what can be achieved in a particular setting such as a school or unit?
- How far does the location of the setting determine what can be done?
- What is the relationship between what is going on in the setting and what is being offered to contemporaries in primary and secondary schools?

One of the greatest increases in special educational provision in recent years has been in various forms of peripatetic teaching and advisory services. Their purpose has been to improve special educational arrangements within primary and secondary schools, to support the work of teachers in those schools and to provide specialist individual and small group teaching. Again there are questions to be asked which include:

- How much effort goes into trying to improve the work of schools and teachers as a whole?
- Are attempts to achieve general improvements coordinated with those of other subject and phase advisers and inspectors?
- What priorities inform the use of available or special education teacher time?
- What proportion of time is given to preparing materials, to planning with other teachers, to counselling and supporting children in general and to various forms of support and withdrawal teaching?
- What are the criteria used to evaluate these services and who evaluates them?

The general contention is that all these questions are being answered in very general terms. There is little differentiation in the level or intensity of what is on offer. The location of special education is taken to imply levels of knowledge, skill, resource and time which are not questioned. There is at present no framework within which to make an analysis of the nature and degree of special educational provision being made either for an individual or in a particular form of provision.

The Service-Delivery Model

The original medical model assumed a very crude division between first aid in primary and secondary school and hospital treatment in special schools. A similar division was later reflected in the arbitrary distinction between 'remedial' and 'special education' which developed in the 1950s and 1960s.

Although this began to break down as a more well resourced units and classes were established in primary and secondary schools, each form of provision was set up separately, often under different management, with little understanding of the common features in the work. For example, units for disturbed children were placed under different management from units and schools for children with emotional and behaviour difficulties.

The perception of special education as a service requires that the focus of attention moves from *where* special education is provided to *what* is being delivered. It demands the greater specification of the levels of service that can be offered in terms of the degree to which the normal process of education is supplemented or replaced by special provision. This in turn demands the development of a unified support service to schools and colleges which specifies what it can deliver, where, how often and at what cost. The rest of the book is addressed to outlining a framework within which to describe how these demands may be met.

Notes

1. *Special Educational Needs* (The Warnock Report), Cmnd 7212, HMSO, 1978.
2. Education Act 1981, HMSO.
3. *The National Curriculum: A Consultation Document*, Department of Education and Science, 1987.
4. 'Disability and Restricted Opportunity', Monograph No 1, OECD/CERI, 1986.
5. DES Circular 8/81 Education Act 1981.
6. DES Circular 1/83 Assessments and Statements of Special Educational Needs 1983.
7. *From Coping to Confidence*, Department of Education and Science, NFER, 1982.

8. B. Goacher, P. Evans, J. Welton and K. Wedell, *Policy and Provision for Special Educational Needs: Implementing the 1981 Education Act*, Cassell, 1988

9. S. Jowett, S. Hegarty and D. Moses, *Joining Forces: A Study of Links between Ordinary and Special Schools*, NFER/Nelson, 1988.

10. S. Hegarty and D. Moses, *Developing Expertise: Inset for Special Educational Needs*, NFER/Nelson, 1988.

11. D. Moses, S. Hegarty, and S. Jowelt, *Supporting Ordinary Schools: LEA Initiatives*, NFER/Nelson, 1988.

12. *Educational Opportunities for All?*, (The Fish Report), ILEA, 1985.

CHAPTER 2

Definitions of Special Education

From Treatment to Education

The history of special education would be much poorer without the contribution of health service professionals. It was often a medical initiative which led to education and training for children and young people with disabilities. Nevertheless, one of the significant changes to have taken place since the 1940s is a move away from the medical direction and specification of special education. Provision previously described as treatment, with its medical connotation, is now described in educational terms.

The Education Act 1944[1] was the first to incorporate provision for 'handicapped' children within general educational legislation and the medical model was still the dominant one. The phrase used to describe provision in that Act was 'special educational treatment' and a medical examination was the only legal requirement for determining whether special educational provision was necessary. 'Special educational treatment' remained the legal definition until the 1981 Act was passed. The words used in the 1944 Act reflect the thinking at the time.

> It shall be the duty of every local education authority to ascertain what children in their area require special educational treatment . . . The authority may require the parent of any child who has attained the age of two years . . . to submit the child for examination by a medical officer of the authority for advice as to whether the child suffering from any disability of mind or body and as to the extent of such disability . . .
>
> (Section 34)

The use of the word 'ascertainment' became charged with the same negative overtones as 'certification'. Pupils were ascertained by a medical examination which placed them into categories of handicap. The Act clearly envisaged handicaps as arising directly from individual deficits and disabilities:

> If, after considering the advice given . . . the authority decide that the child is suffering from a disability of mind of such a nature or to such an extent as to make him incapable of receiving education at school. . .
>
> (Section 56)

Although the concept of education was broadening there were limits. In a chicken and egg way definitions of mental deficiency implied an inability to profit from education and a marked lack of ability to respond to education was seen as one of the criteria defining mental deficiency:

> The minister shall make regulations defining the several categories of pupils requiring special educational treatment and making provision as to the special methods appropriate to the education of pupils in each category.
>
> (Section 33)

With the new confidence in intelligence testing and diagnosis it was clear that children requiring special educational treatment could be categorised. Subsequent experience was to show that few children had a single disability and in many instances categorisation was far from simple. It soon became apparent that individual responses to disability were very varied.

> The arrangements made by the local education authority for the special educational treatment of pupils of any such category shall, so far as is practicable, provide for the education of pupils in whose case the disability is serious in special schools appropriate to that category, but where that is impracticable, or where the disability is not serious, the arrangements may provide for the giving of any such education in any school maintained or assisted by the local education authority.
>
> (Section 34)

The Act continued the tradition that separate provision in special schools was the best form of provision. In some ways these schools were seen as having the same status as hospitals. They were places where children were either to be cured of learning difficulties or cared for in a safe environment away from the rigours of primary and secondary schools.

Although, with hindsight, it is easy to be critical of the 1944 definitions they were at the time a considerable advance on previous legislation. The central features of special educational arrangements were consistent with the educational philosophy of the time. Categorisation was not confined only to those with disabilities. All children could be sorted out into grammar, technical and secondary modern material at the age of eleven. Within the thinking of the time children with special educational needs were being given access to the education system and provision for them was clearly the responsibility of local education authorities.

From the Act to Warnock

In summary, the duties of local education authorities, as a result of the 1944 Act, included finding out which children were handicapped and providing special educational treatment for them in special schools and elsewhere. Decisions about the need for such treatment were based primarily on medical reports which diagnosed handicaps and placed children in one of a number of categories. These were thought to represent groups of individuals with the same needs. It was also supposed that there would be a particular methodology appropriate for each category. The concept of education, although broad, still assumed a level of ability before children could profit from it, with some children considered to be ineducable.

The Act encouraged local education authorities to get other advice in addition to a medical report and over the years the reports of teachers and educational psychologists were given increasing weight by authorities. However, for statutory procedures, such as declaring a child to be unable to profit from education, the medical report was the only legal requirement.

There was increasing dissatisfaction with the notion of ineducability, and with children being deprived of the right to education, during the 1960s. The idea of education as any planned and systematic intervention to facilitate learning gained ground. New legislation was enacted. The Education Act 1970,[2] which came into force in 1971, abolished the legal status of ineducability and made local education authorities responsible for educational provision for all children, whatever the nature or degree of their disabilities. In effect it established the right of all children to education.

There continued to be dissatisfaction with current special education procedures as well as an increasing interest in making more provision for those who were disabled within primary and secondary schools. Integration became a major topic of discussion. It was against this background that the government of the day agreed to set up a committee of enquiry. The Warnock Committee, as it became known, was given a wide brief and took four years to complete its work. Its report *Special Educational Needs* was widely welcomed.

The Warnock Committee Definitions

The Warnock Committee brought together the current thinking of the 1970s. It reflected changes in the concepts of intelligence, testing and of handicap which resulted in much less certainty that children could be neatly categorised in terms of disability or intelligence. The Committee recognised a continuum of special educational needs, from mild to severe and profound, in a single school population. The Report's definitions of needs and provision were:

> In very broad terms special educational need is likely to take the form of the need for one or more of the following:
>
> (i) the provision of special means of access to the curriculum through special equipment, facilities or resources, modification of the physical environment or specialist teaching techniques;
> (ii) the provision of a special or modified curriculum;
> (iii) particular attention to the social structure and emotional climate in which education takes place.
>
> (Paragraph 3.19)

Special educational needs were individual and they were defined for the first time in terms of the curriculum, the means of access to it and the social and emotional environment in which it was taught. The Report stated:

> We propose that special educational provision for the children with whom we are concerned should, therefore, be understood in terms of one or more broad criteria:
>
> (i) effective access on a full or part-time basis to teachers with appropriate qualifications or substantial experience or both;
> (ii) effective access on a full or part-time basis to other professionals with appropriate training;
> and
> (iii) an appropriate educational and physical environment with the necessary equipment and resources appropriate to the child's needs.
>
> (Paragraph 3.40)

Provision was also to be made in individual terms and related to assessed needs. It was defined in terms of professional skills, technology and environmental factors.

These definitions, which represented major changes in thinking about needs and provision, were widely accepted in principle. Although many of the recommendations of the report were not implemented these definitions were substantially reflected in those of the Education Act 1981.

The Education Act 1981

In that Act, which came into force in 1983, special educational needs were defined for the first time in relative terms. They were seen as learning difficulties of all kinds rather than as individual deficits. Special educational needs were seen as arising from physical, sensory or intellectual disabilities and not as identical with them. The 1981 Act's definitions are

> For the purposes of this Act a child has 'special educational needs' if he has a learning difficulty which calls for special educational provision to be made for him.
>
> (Section 1)
>
> . . . a child has a 'learning difficulty' if –
>
> (a) he has a significantly greater difficulty in learning than the majority of children of his age; or
> (b) he has a disability which either prevents or hinders him from making use of educational facilities of a kind generally provided in schools, within the area of the local authority concerned, for children of his age; or
> (c) he is under the age of five years and is, or would be if special educational provision were not made for him, likely to fall within paragraph (a) or (b) when over that age.
>
> (Section 2)

The use of the term 'learning difficulty' has subsequently caused concern. It was intended in the psychological sense that all behaviour is learned, including difficult behaviour, and that only when physical and sensory disabilities give rise to learning difficulties is there a need for special education.

The use of the term 'learning difficulty' with the qualifications 'moderate' and 'severe' to denote what was previously described as educational subnormality has led to confusion. Those working with children with emotional and behaviour difficulties have thought the definition inappropriate. Many other professional and voluntary organisations are uncomfortable with a broad and relative definition, particularly in the absence of any guidance about its interpretation.

> 'Special educational provision' means –
>
> (a) in relation to a child who has attained the age of two years, educational provision which is additional to, or different from, the educational provision made generally for children of his age in schools maintained by the local authority concerned; and,
> (b) in relation to any child under that age, educational provision of any kind.
>
> (Section 3)

The major advance was to define special educational provision in educational terms. But this has presented difficulties in respect to the provision of treatments and services, for example speech therapy, which are not managed by local education authorities. Two conflicting trends have not yet been reconciled: the increased inter-disciplinary working in many areas of special education and the development of appropriate specific educational programmes for individuals. The Act reflects the latter but makes the former more difficult to develop.

After the Act

The definitions show how the move from treatment to education has been expressed in legislation and reports over a period of about forty years. However, the changes are not always reflected in common practice. There is a natural tendency to group children for administrative purposes which conflicts with a wish to individualise provision. There remains a strong medical influence which tends to be expressed in an ever increasing number of educational therapies which are seen as qualitively different from aspects of the special educational curriculum. Music therapy, for example, is considered to be of a higher status than music teaching. But above all there is not yet a clear idea of what it means to provide an individual with special education. What are the parameters of such provision? It may be helpful, at this point, to look briefly at the array of informed and lay opinion about the Act's definitions which occurs in the evidence to the House of Commons Committee.

The House of Commons Education, Science and Arts Committee

This Committee undertook a review of the 1981 Education Act at the beginning of 1987. Its work was seriously curtailed by the proroguing of Parliament in May of that year. The work of all such committees ceases until a new parliament is elected and a new committee set up. A short report[3] was published but in the subsequent flurry of consultation papers about educational reform the impression could be gained that special education has ceased to exist.

It is evident, if legislation is to last and not be changed in every parliament, that it should provide an enabling framework within which to work. Evidence to the Committee indicated that the 1981 Act framework has been a positive influence on the development of special education. Major changes were not recommended but many submissions sought guidance and clarification.

The Department of Education and Science appears to have shown a singular lack of enthusiasm for giving appropriate guidance. Soon after the Act was passed the Department commissioned three important research studies into the implementation of the Act.[4, 5, 6, 7] Local authorities have shown a very varied response and a need for guidance. Their existence,   however, has served as adequate grounds for Departmental inactivity.

The evidence to the House of Commons Education, Science and Arts Committee shows that there is still confusion about the interpretation of the Act's definitions six years after the Act was passed and four years after its implementation. Although it is recognised that, with relative definitions, provision will vary from school to school and area to area, central questions remain unanswered. One of the most important is, what constitutes that which is additional to, or different from, provision generally available within schools run by a local educational authority?

Evidence presented to the Committee on the question of definition was largely coloured by whether special interest groups found them helpful to their objectives. On the one hand they were described as positive, satisfactory, beneficial, helpful, constructive and defining a useful concept. On the other they were thought to be too broad, imprecise, circular, vague and unclear with respect to whether they covered the wider range of special educational needs (the 20 per cent suggested in the Warnock Report). There was widespread support for the intention of the definitions and their generally positive influence but considerable doubt about their usefulness in practice in the absence of much clearer central guidance.

Conclusion

Legal definitions have changed and are much less precise. They are now more concerned with what an individual needs rather than with putting him or her in a category. But the relativity of the definitions and limited experience of their use is currently resulting in uncertainty. It is suggested that there is no case for legal definitions which are more specific but there is clear evidence of the need for interpretation and guidance if there is to be equity in provision from authority to authority.

However good legal definitions are, it is still necessary to interpret them. Operational definitions are necessary at national and local levels in order to plan services and estimate the resources involved. It is with the conceptual framework on which to base these operational definitions that the following chapters will deal.

Notes

1. Education Act 1944, HMSO.
2. Education (Handicapped Children) Act 1970, HMSO.
3. House of Commons Education, Science and Arts Committee, *Third Report*, Vols I and II, HMSO, 1987.
4. B. Goacher, P. Evans, J. Welton and K. Wedell, *Policy and Provision for Special Educational Needs: Implementing the 1981 Education Act*, Cassell 1988.
5. S. Jowett, S. Hegarty, and D. Moses, *Joining Forces: A Study of Links between Ordinary and Special Schools*, NFER/Nelson, 1988.
6. S. Hegarty, and D. Moses, *Developing Expertise: Inset for Special Educational Needs*, NFER/Nelson, 1988.
7. D. Moses, S. Hegarty, and S. Jowett, *Supporting Ordinary Schools: LEA Initiatives*, NFER/Nelson, 1988.

CHAPTER 3

Situations, Resources and Responses

Legal and administrative definitions of special educational needs and provision afford a general framework and philosophy; but every day practices require more precise guidelines. Given broad definitions of provision, and an indication of teaching time available to meet them, what kinds of provision should be encouraged? This chapter will use current descriptions and examples of available resources as a basis for identifying the major parameters of what might reasonably be described as special education.

The relativity of current definitions causes particular problems. The points at which learning difficulties become 'significant' and provision 'additional or different' have to be determined pragmatically by each local education authority and each primary and secondary school. These points, which may vary from authority to authority, and from school to school, will be determined by objectives priorities and the use of resources. Thus the number of special educational needs which arise in a local educational authority area may be determined by the general staffing, support and resources of schools in that area. Similarly the number of special educational needs in a school is related to the quality of education provided for all children in that school.

In recent years many changes have taken place in special schools and classes. Individual assessment and programme planning have become more prescriptive and aspects of curricular development more systematic. But while what goes on may be more precisely planned, most descriptions of special educational provision remain very general and unspecific. Recommendations after assessment are usually very broad and the choices offered relate to location, and what is available, rather than to what is needed.

During the same period there has been a marked increase in the number of special education teachers working in an advisory and support capacity. Many of them have become caught up in attempting to help schools improve as a whole, with the intention of reducing the incidence of special educational needs. This may be at the expense of helping schools to improve their ability to identify and meet special educational needs. The relative priority given, by a professional or a service, to changing the context and to helping to meet the special educational needs, which arise from that context, needs to be determined. Again job descriptions are vague and services very loosely described. Services must be more precise about the different types of support they can give to children with different kinds of special educational needs.

What is Special Educational Provision?

When a group of special education teachers was asked to describe special educational provision the following list emerged. Although the priority given to items varied according to whether individuals worked in primary or secondary schools, in a support teaching service or in special schools or units, an agreed list emerged as follows:

- curriculum development and modification;
- the assessment of individuals and situations;
- programme development for individuals and small groups;
- providing a protected environment;
- providing equipment, materials and resources;
- advice and counselling;
- specialist teaching;
- collaborative teaching;
- contributing to in-service education programmes;
- working with parents; and
- liaison with other professionals.

As can be seen the list was a very general one. Broad descriptions of activities, capable of many different interpretations, were given. For example, 'work with parents' is a common element in many job descriptions but such a phrase does not indicate what is done, for how long it is done and what resources might be involved in doing it.

The many possible kinds of work with parents can include:

- giving parents information about the school's programme;
- home visiting to see the child's family background;

- seeing that home-school diaries are kept;
- supervising a home teaching programme; and
- counselling parents in respect of their children's disabilities and difficulties.

Work with parents is, thus, a loose non-specific description. It fails to distinguish between supervising parental participation in programmes and working with parents to help them understand their involvement in their children's difficulties and to contribute to overcoming them. Each of the specific activities outlined has different time and resource implications. The kind of work appropriate with particular parents of particular children should be specified as part of a comprehensive assessment, as should the resources involved. Itemising 'work with parents' is an illustration of the need for a much more precise descriptive system.

Special Educational Provision in Primary Schools

Just as descriptions of work can be loose so can the descriptions of provision. This is illustrated by looking at two typical situations.

Table 3.1

	School A	School B
Number on roll	230	214
Staffing	Head + 11	Head + 8
	2 NTAs	1 NTA
Children with SEN	32	59
SEN teaching time (hrs) from school staff	7½	15
LEA provision	P Hg Unit	+ 2NTA for
	(2T + 1NTA)	children with
		statements
External resources		
Support teacher (hrs/term)	15	12
Peripatetic/Language Teacher (hrs/term)	15	
Educational Psychologist (visits/term)	2	2–3

(NTA = non-teaching assistant, P Hg = Partially hearing, SEN = Special educational needs)

Table 3.1 gives details of the resources available to meet special educational needs in two primary schools in 1987. In School A the total staffing includes the staff in the unit for partially hearing children. The additional non-teaching assistant time in School B is related to the specific needs of children who are the subject of statements.

In School A there was a total of between 8½ and 9 hours a week available for meeting the needs of 32 children who had been indicated as in need of additional help. There was also about 1½ hours a week for speech and language work and perhaps some support and help from the teachers in the unit for partially hearing children.

In School B there were about 15 hours a week for work with 59 children assessed as in need of additional help. There was an additional hour a week for support teaching and regular visiting by the educational psychologist. The two non-teaching assistants were employed to work with four children who were the subject of statements. Whether they provided any support for other children in the school was not clear.

When a group was asked to say how the available resources might best be used the following statements emerged. Resources would be used:

- to develop and supply appropriate teaching materials;
- to carry out joint assessment with class teachers;
- to plan, together with class teachers, programmes for individual children;
- to carry out collaborative and support teaching; and
- to withdraw children for specialist teaching.

All these general aims are very acceptable. Nevertheless, as with 'work with parents', there is little precision. Admittedly it is difficult to be precise in a training exercise which lacks the subtleties of a real situation. But there was no approximate time allocation or identification of where and when support teaching or withdrawal might be appropriate. However, it has to be said that the tools to carry out a more detailed analysis are not readily available.

Special Educational Provision in Secondary Schools

A similar exercise with material from secondary schools resulted in slightly more precision. Two concrete examples of secondary schools and their resources for meeting special educational needs are set out in table 3.2.

The schools were in different counties and the resources available illustrate the variation which exists both in authority staffing levels and the ways in which schools allocate resources.

One solution suggested for the use of the time available in School B was based on the use of time in a 20-session week. The allocation of teacher time (in hours) is set out in Table 3.3.

Table 3.2

	School A	School B
Number on roll	1,350	870
Staffing	Head + 90 (+ 2 PT)	Head + 48
Children with SEN	73	Net specified
School SE time	2 FT + ⅓	3 FT equivalent
LEA provision		
P Hg Unit	1 FT and 1 PT	2 FT
	(9 children)	(10 children)
Support teaching (hr/month)	Nil	2
Educational Psychologist visits	2/term	3 hr/month

(P Hg = Partially hearing, FT = full-time teacher, PT = Part-time teacher)

Table 3.3

Tasks	HOD	Teacher 2	Teacher 3
Withdrawal teaching	1	1	1
Collaborative			
assessment and teaching	9	13	13
Outreach work with parents and professionals	2	2	2
Resource and curriculum development	2	2	2
Management	2	—	—
Staff development	3	1	1
Preparation/liaison	1	1	1

(HOD = Head of development)

Here priorities are expressed in the allocation of time. They were also expressed in support teaching priorities, namely to provide such teaching in English and mathematics periods rather than in other subjects, given the available resources. But tasks are very general, with for example, outreach with parents and professionals being unspecified in nature. As has already been shown, work with parents can vary widely in kind, depth and resource implications.

Ideas About Special Education

The illustrations show that it is not a simple task to describe what is done in the name of special education. Since the 1944 Act the main focus has changed from treatment to education and from categorical programmes to individual curriculum variation. Its relationship to regular education has become relative and the timespan over which it is provided has increased. Nevertheless its nature has not yet been satisfactorily described.

It is possible to discern two contrasting ideas in much that is written and said about special education. On the one hand it is argued that it is a separate field in which children with handicaps are given a very special kind of education while being protected from the rigours of primary and secondary schools. On the other hand it is maintained that special education is just 'good education'. Ideally, with well trained teachers, and a philosophy of non-segregation, all individual needs will be met within a school which provides appropriate education for all.

The first idea is more common among special educators. While it gives due weight to the special educational needs arising from particular disabilities it may overrate the special skills required to meet them. Such a view may have a positive value in maintaining morale and endorsing the value of work done by special education teachers. However, it gives rise to a number of implicit assumptions, often encouraged by those working in the field, which need to be questioned.

The second view may underrate the special skills associated with teaching children with a particular disability. It is most often held by primary and secondary school teachers sensitive to individual differences in learning style and pace. It argues that much of the time of special education teachers is taken up with doing things a reasonable school or a reasonable teacher should have done. It questions whether special education should exist and implies that 'good' education subsumes special education, because it can meet all children's needs.

This is a helpful aspiration which can do much to reduce unnecessary segregation by recognising needs common to all children. While it is not an approach which appeals to the hard pressed class or subject teacher, who has a number of children whose needs are difficult to meet, it is consistent with a relative definition of special need.

Implicit Assumptions

A number of untested assumptions are often made about special education. It may be helpful to look at three of them. These are that:

- any work by teachers with special educational qualifications is by definition special education;
- what goes on in special education classrooms is special education; and
- grouping children by disabilities and by special educational needs in itself defines special educational provision.

If we wish to investigate the nature of special education it is important to question these assumptions.

Teacher Qualifications

The first assumption implies that how a teacher is described is more important in defining special education than what he or she does. Questioning the first assumption involves looking at the borderline between the competences expected of all primary and secondary school teachers and those expected of special education teachers. It is a borderline which is difficult to define as some skills, such as those involved in the early stages of assessment, previously confined to the special field are now expected of all teachers.

Nevertheless, initial and in-service education must make some assumptions about the nature and the levels of the skills they are aiming to develop. With such skills as assessment, task analysis, target setting and programme planning there will continue to be a shifting borderline between the general competence expected of all teachers and the degree of specific proficiency to be expected of special education teachers.

Location

The second assumption is that what goes on in special schools, and in special education classrooms of all kinds, is always by definition special education. In other words, special education is defined by location rather than curriculum or programme. As the separation between special education and primary and secondary education has decreased, and a wider range of special educational needs recognised, the curriculum is one area where there is increased common ground. How special is the teaching and the programme in classes and groups labelled special?

The relationship between the curriculum and individual programmes on offer to all children of a particular age and those on offer to children deemed to have special educational needs is a crucial determinant of the nature of special education. It involves looking at the relationship between what is taught and the way it is taught in primary and secondary schools and in special education classes and groups. Too great a difference may itself be handicapping, while too little difference may be equally so. In any case a definition of special education by location is inadequate.

Grouping

The third assumption is an administrative rather than an educational one. Putting groups of children with the same disabilities, or the same kinds of learning difficulties, together for teaching purposes may be thought to define special education. In other words the group is more important in defining special education than what is provided for them.

Although common and traditional, the answers to the questions who, where and with whom are not sufficient to define special education. It is necessary to look more closely at the nature of the special education process.

A Relative Baseline

While it is true that high expectations improve performance it is equally true that education has suffered from a belief that the performance of the outstandingly successful teacher can be replicated in the work of all teachers through in-service training. It has also suffered from a naive belief that the average hard working teacher is readily able to incorporate new material, methods and knowledge into his or her daily work.

The relative concept of special educational need and provision introduced by the 1981 Act has already been mentioned. Although relativity causes considerable confusion to those who like tidy, simplistic solutions, the great advantage is that as general teaching proficiency and resources increase fewer children need be labelled as having special educational needs. We may hope that more and more aspects of 'good education' will become more generally available.

It is important to identify positive attributes of special education and to avoid seeing it simply as provision which solves problems created by lack of knowledge, ineffective teaching and inadequate care for the individual pupil.

The greatest difficulty which arises from the concept of relativity is how to define the characteristics of a reasonable educational programme generally available in schools in a local education authority area. What should be the attributes of special education which are additional to, or different from, the education generally available to all pupils in primary and secondary schools in that area?

This leads naturally to the identification of general characteristics of schools as a baseline. Those below represent a list of general and desirable attributes and reasonable expectations:

1. Schools should have written statements of their curriculum and of the objectives that they expect to achieve in each subject area at different ages.
2. Teachers should work to those objectives and plan their teaching programmes in such a way that individual tasks and objectives are clear.
3. Schools should have a pupil record system which enables teachers to

know what individual children have experienced and mastered and which provides a basis on which they can plan their teaching programmes.

4. Schools and teachers should maintain regular contact with all parents and engage in a continuous dialogue about individual progress.
5. Schools should be familiar with the available range of educational, health and social services available to them and with the limits of what they have to offer.
6. Schools and teachers should be able to take the first steps in identifying and assessing the most common special educational needs of all kinds.
7. Schools should have a written statement of what they can and do provide to meet the most common special educational needs which arise.

Preventing or Meeting Needs

One of the major problems for special educators, particularly when working in or supporting primary and secondary schools, is the undue demands made by schools where curriculum, materials and management may be poor. Such schools ask for the most help from supporting and peripatetic services and often refer the most children for special educational provision elsewhere.

Where should special education services draw a line between inappropriate problems of school management, which are the concern of governors and local authorities, and the needs of individuals with learning difficulties? For example, where a school appears to have above 15–20 per cent of its population exhibiting special educational needs, whose is the primary responsibility? Is this a question about the management of the school as a whole, which should be tackled by the authority's general advisory service, or is it a problem to be tackled by providing special education services? There must be a point in the dynamic development of many schools where the extent of special need requires general action and not additional special educational services.

The dilemma of how much time should be devoted to attempting to change the context for the better and how much to directly helping children identified as having special educational needs has already been noted. The less effective the school the more it needs changing and the greater the number of children who need help. However, changing the context or improving schools is a task shared with other advisory services and special educators have to fit into a more general framework of school evaluation.

Appraisal, Preparation and Action

Appraising the situation, preparing working conditions within the school and taking one of a variety of actions represent different aspects of the work of a number of educational professionals who work with schools. All those concerned with children with special educational needs have to consider these three aspects of their contacts with schools. Whether they are educational psychologists, special education advisors, peripatetic teachers or teachers in special schools doing outreach work the same principles apply.

What are the objectives of *all* those responsible for inspecting and advising primary and secondary schools? Are their objectives compatible? It is important to know whether they are giving advice consistent with mitigating and meeting special educational needs. Special educators need to know how their objectives relate to those of their colleagues in other advisory services.

The appraising of educational contexts, whether of schools as a whole or classes, is a process which special education teachers share. Changing contexts to prevent some special educational needs arising is also a task shared with other advisors and inspectors. All too often different support services work in isolation from each other and from other advisory services. Changing contexts is not an activity unique to special educators and is therefore not a distinctive characteristic of special education.

Appraisal

There are broadly four different aspects to be appraised: the work of the school as a whole; the teaching of particular subjects or aspects of the curriculum; the work of particular classes; and the performance of individuals or groups of children.

The first three of these are tasks shared with all other advisors, advisory and peripatetic teachers working in the authority. Only the appraisal of children in order to assess their special educational needs, and to suggest provision if it exists is exclusive to special educators and this responsibility is shared with class and subject teachers.

Whether or not the appraisal of schools as a whole and of subject and class teaching, with respect to meeting special educational needs, is well coordinated with that of other interests, the process takes time. It has to be recognised that time has to be spent in appraisal and assessment before appropriate action can be taken. Job descriptions and resource allocations have to take this into account.

Preparation

Having appraised the needs of schools, teaching situations, teachers and above all of the children concerned, it cannot be assumed that appropriate conditions exist in the school for actions of all kinds. Again, preparation may be an activity shared with others at the four levels outlined for appraisal: the whole school, the subject, the class and with respect to children with special educational needs. For example, if in-service education is planned this has to be coordinated within an overall programme.

The reason for identifying this phase is again because of its resource implications. Preparation for service delivery is an important element in resource use in the early stages of the introduction of new procedures. It is yet another demand on the time of special educators. To meet this demand may mean having less time for actual provision.

Action

What do we wish to do to help children with special educational needs? How do we describe the ways in which special educational needs are met? These are questions which it is hoped will be easier to answer after considering the nature of special education in more detail.

Conclusion

This chapter has looked at the very general way in which special education is described. It also recognises that before special education can be provided effectively, particularly in primary and secondary schools, the borderline with regular education has to be defined in collaboration with other advisors and inspectors.

Because the two phases of appraisal and preparation come first in the logical sequence most attention has been focused on them. The action phase is the one on which the following sections and chapters of this book will concentrate.

CHAPTER 4

Dimensions and Levels

Working from the baseline of general provision in schools it begins to be possible to build up a picture of the characteristics or dimensions of special educational provision and to consider those dimensions in terms of the degree of intervention or level of resources required.

The term dimension, rather than parameter, is used because special educational provision is on a continuum with regular education: where its attributes increasingly modified as children's special educational needs become more complex.

Along each dimension it is suggested that there should be a number of levels to define more precisely what is being done. The levels suggested in this book are illustrative. It is only possible to decide what levels of intervention are practicable in the light of the provision and resources available in a particular authority or school.

An Array of Dimensions

Having described dimensions or characteristics it is necessary to determine the dimensions that are necessary and sufficient to define special education. In the following paragraphs 16 dimensions are defined and briefly described. They are seen as providing a framework for the more precise definition of provision. In subsequent chapters each will be discussed in terms of levels of intervention, envisaged as points on a continuum from the typical manifestation of the characteristic in regular education to more and more specialised variations of it.

Dimension 1: The Curriculum
The most obvious example of a dimension is the degree of curriculum variation necessary for different degrees of special educational need. The curriculum is now a central feature of special education. In some respects it is now the only one to which particular attention is being given. Given that there is a standard or common curriculum for primary and secondary schools, then there may be a need for more and more modification or variation the greater the degree of complexity of a child's learning difficulties. This may range from assistance to follow the standard curriculum to a significantly different variation of that curriculum for those with profound and multiple degrees of intellectual disability.

Dimension 2: The Environment
There are few special educational needs where the environment is not a factor in their genesis. The environment may also form a significant element in meeting such needs. There are very obvious examples, such as acoustic environments to assist children with hearing impairments. The environment is also a significant factor in the management of emotional and behaviour problems. This continuum is related to some extent to that of technology. The dimension may range from the regular classroom to a highly specialised residential environment.

Dimension 3: Technology
Technology of all kinds has always had a significant place in special education and new micro-technological advances promise increasingly sophisticated help for children and young people with disabilities and significant difficulties. They include aids to communication, the means of gaining access to and managing information, word processing, aids to mobility and methods of environmental control. Individuals can be assisted by appropriate levels of technology from simple equipment to complex aids to living and learning. This dimension covers a continuum from access to the technology used in the education of all children to very specialised applications for individuals.

Dimension 4: Relationships
If children are to function in the community as adults then those with and without disabilities and significant difficulties need to be aware of each other and develop skills in making relationships with each other. This is as true for the child who is blind as for the child with a marked degree of intellectual disability and for a child with an emotional disorder as for one with a physical disability. Special education has been noted for its attention to the relationships of teachers with children and of children

with each other within special schools and classes. The need to promote and foster relationships within neighbouring schools and within the community is now receiving more attention. The relationships of children with special educational needs with their contemporaries cannot be left to chance. This dimension involves a continuum from regular unplanned interaction to carefully planned situations designed to encourage interaction.

Time

Time has already been discussed in terms of the demands on teachers of appraisal and preparation before special education can be delivered. Time is also related to the delivery of special education.

The time conceived in the following dimensions is specialist time as distinct from generalist time. This distinction has to be made for two reasons: teachers with special education responsibilities in primary and secondary schools may spend some time giving 'regular' education; second, much provision now being made for individual children in primary and secondary schools is in the form of additional teaching and non-teaching sessions. These may be given by people who may have no relevant experience, receive no appropriate training, and have no regular support from special educators. It is questionable whether such assistance should be described as special educational provision, although it may be considered to be 'additional' in terms of the Act.

The time dimensions outlined here are intended to represent access to appropriately trained or experienced teachers, as originally envisaged in the Warnock Report. The two dimensions are intended to represent the time given by special education teachers, directly or indirectly, to children who need their assistance. They are:

Dimension 5: The Time Intensity of Provision
This reflects the proportion of special education teaching time devoted to individuals and groups within a given timespan. Time intensity may range from support at relatively long intervals, through monthly supervision and weekly teaching sessions to 24-hour care and education.

Dimension 6: The Time Duration
It is common to estimate how long a form of provision is thought to be necessary or to say how long provision is going to be made before a review. This characteristic of special education may range from the short term, in terms of weeks or months, to provision necessary for most of a child's school life.

Dimension 7: The Contact Type
This dimension describes the nature of the special educator's contact with a child or group of children, which may be indirect or direct. At one end of the range may be distant consultant support, where the special education teacher works through the child's regular teacher and may have no regular direct contact with the child. At another level might be small group teaching by a special educator, while at the other end of the range might be 24-hour teaching and care in a residential setting. This dimension has time implications for special educators; it also involves assumptions about the contributions to be made by the primary and secondary school teachers with whom they may work.

Professional Knowledge and Skills

Knowledge and skills are often seen as an inextricable element in a special educator's armoury. There seems to be a case for separating the two attributes since it is not always necessary to have a wide or deep knowledge of the special educational implications of a disability in order to be of help to an individual. For example a person skilled in signing and finger spelling can be of great assistance as an interpreter. The increased availability of non-teaching assistants working under direction implies a differentiation of some of the skills of programming and management from some of the skills involved in working with children. Thus it is suggested that there are two dimensions.

Dimension 8: Professional Knowledge
This characteristic may range from the minimum knowledge to be expected of all teachers to the expert knowledge necessary to educate children with multiple and complex disabilities.

Dimension 9: Professional Skills
Non-teaching assistants working with teachers, as well as teachers themselves, may need particular skills to work with individual children. The skills concerned may range from those effective with minor and common special educational needs to those required to work with children with severe and complex problems.

Dimension 10: Supporting Educational Professional Contributions
This dimension describes the contribution of educational psychologists and educational social workers who work with schools in support of special educational provision. The work of both professions with parents, and their vital contributions to assessment, are well known. Psychologists also make a significant contribution to programme

planning and to evaluation. However, the direct contributions to special education are less well defined. This dimension is intended to represent a continuum of involvement with children and their families which can be interpreted as providing special education as distinct from assessing need for it or evaluating its effectiveness.

Supporting Health and Social Service Contributions

It is neither possible, nor indeed sensible, to consider provision solely in terms of what those employed by the education service may provide. They cannot work in isolation from professionals in other services if a child's needs are to be met comprehensively. The contributions of the health and social services may be significant. There is no intention here to define these for the professional concerned. The outlines below are intended solely as illustrations of ways in which the contributions of those services might also be considered in terms of levels within a multi-disciplinary approach to meeting special educational needs. It is suggested that there are four additional dimensions of special education which relate to these services.

Dimension 11: Health Service Treatment and Supervision
Although medical and nursing care is separately managed this dimension includes the degree to which both may be necessary as part of a disabled child's total programme. This may range from the level of oversight necessary for all children to 24-hour medical and nursing care for a small group of children.

Dimension 12: The Provision of Therapy
Speech therapy, physiotherapy and occupational and other therapies may all be important elements in a programme to meet the special educational needs of a child. This dimension represents a continuum based on the frequency of oversight and therapeutic sessions required by different children.

Dimension 13: The Social Service Status of the Child
It is necessary to recognise the social service status of many children with special educational needs. It is also important to recognise that many children coming within the professional concern of social services will have special educational needs. The department's 'parental' responsibilities for the child and the family should include recognising such needs and contributing to meeting them. The dimension might range from whether the family is known to the service through other kinds of oversight and supervision to being in the care of the local authority.

Dimension 14: The Level of Social Service Activity
This dimension is intended to convey the level of work or intervention of social service personnel. This may range from no action to intensive family case work.

Parental Contributions

Parents are encouraged and expected to become involved in their children's education. In the field of special education the aim is a genuine partnership between parents and professionals working with their children. This aspiration, which is hard to achieve, is reflected in two dimensions.

Dimension 15: Parental Involvement
This characteristic represents the degree to which parents are involved in their child's special educational needs. In some instances of learning and behaviour difficulties it is recognised that parent's attitudes, expectations and actions may be part of the problem. This dimension indicates the extent to which special educational provision may need to include planned help for parents which may range from regular but relatively ordinary contacts to family therapy.

Dimension 16: Parental Participation
In recent years a particular feature of special education has been the contribution of parents to their children's education. This dimension covers a range which may include completing home–school diaries, participation in a home teaching programme, and working with teachers in schools and classes.

Summary

It is suggested that each of the 16 dimensions represents a continuum from an attribute of everyday education through an increasing modification of that attribute to the variation necessary to educate a child with the most severe and complex special educational needs. Those outlined briefly in the previous paragraphs are suggested as a possible framework for defining special education more precisely.

The dimensions might be grouped as follows:

Situational
1. Curriculum
2. Environment
3. Technology

4. Relationships
Temporal
5. Time intensity
6. Time duration
Professional teaching
7. Contact type
8. Knowledge
9. Skills
Supporting professional
10. Supporting educational professional contribution
11. Medical supervision
12. Therapy
13. Social service status
14. Social service action
Parental
15. Parental involvement
16. Parental participation.

Levels of intervention

It is not enough to match a specified need with a crude description of provision or even with more clearly defined dimensions. As we saw in looking at work with parents, a wide range of different actions may fall under a general heading. It will be more helpful if actions can be specified in a way which can be costed in time and manpower. As well as defining dimensions it is therefore necessary to analyse each of them in terms of the significant points on each continuum which might constitute a different level of intervention.

The idea of levels of intervention or of service delivery is not new. One example, from the USA, is given in *Special Education – The Way Ahead*[1] and another occurs in the National Association for Remedial Education publication. *Teaching Roles for Special Educational Needs.*[2] Others, no doubt, also occur in the literature. The point here is not to justify the idea by precedent. It is simply to put it forward for serious consideration without in any way suggesting that it is unique.

One example will illustrate what is meant by 'level' in this book. If we take the dimension 'time intensity' it can be looked at as a continuum. The initial level might be 'available for consultation', where the regular teacher is expected to call for support and advice when necessary. The most time-intense form of special education might be that given by a teacher in a residential school. In between there might be levels indicating different numbers of supervision or teaching sessions, each of which will have their specific teacher – time commitments.

Conclusion

This brief chapter outlines a general framework for further discussion. It suggests 16 dimensions considered necessary to describe special education and introduces the notion of levels of intervention. Before turning to a more detailed description of dimensions in the next chapters it is stressed that the dimensions are suggestions and other characteristics may be preferable. What is argued is that a specification of the kind outlined is vital to the future development of special education.

Notes

1. John Fish, *Special Education – The Way Ahead*, Open University Press, 1985.
2. National Association for Remedial Education, *Teaching Roles for Special Educational Needs*, Guidelines No. 6, NARE, 1985.

CHAPTER 5

Major Dimensions of Special Education

The major dimensions of special education have been outlined, together with the idea of levels of intervention. A number of these dimensions are now set out in some detail. They are not discussed in the same order as they were set out in the previous chapter. Each is discussed in terms of levels of intervention along a continuum, the personnel who might be involved and the levels of resource which might be required. An approach of this kind should enable time and other resources to be allocated and managed with more precision, effectiveness and economy. The first dimension analysed is that of curriculum.

The Curriculum

The original notion of categories of handicap was associated with the idea that each category needed a particular curriculum and methodology. As a result special schools were isolated from the main stream of primary and secondary curriculum development.

One of the major consequences of moving from a treatment to an educational model is the emphasis which is rightly placed on the curriculum. A much closer relationship between the curricula of primary, secondary and special schools is now recognised. This is the consequence of an increasing acceptance that:

- all children are entitled to the same educational opportunities;
- special educational needs are relative; and

- there is a need to make provision to meet special educational needs in primary and secondary schools.

Curricula in special educational provision are now seen as variations derived from the curriculum for all children.

Guidelines issued by the Department of Education and Science suggest that three variants of the general curriculum might be appropriate for children with different kinds of special educational need.
These are broadly as follows:

1. the curriculum followed by all pupils of the same age; special education in this instance relates to the technical support and presentation of material that is necessary to make the curriculum accessible;
2. a modified curriculum where individuals study the same range of subjects as their contemporaries but the objectives set and the methods and materials used are modified; and
3. a special curriculum with emphasis on social and life skills for those with the most severe and complex special educational needs.

This formulation is limited, general and closely tied to the traditional situations in which special education has taken place. At present its application to the assessment of individuals and its resource implications are difficult to specify. A much more rigorous analysis is necessary. That analysis should be one of the significant factors in determining where the special education a child requires can be provided. It is suggested that it requires further development to bring it into line with a national curriculum framework.

The Curriculum Dimension

An alternative formulation might have six steps indicating an increasing distance from the national curriculum to be followed by the majority of the children of the same age.
These might be:

1. technical support to follow a national core curriculum;
2. supplementary teaching to enable the national core curriculum to be followed perhaps over a longer timespan;
3. selective involvement in the national core curriculum together with other elements of a broad and modified curriculum with the same range of subjects as the national curriculum;
4. selective involvement in other curriculum areas not within the national framework which are provided for children of the same age together with other curriculum areas modified in content and objectives;
5. a modified curriculum with the same range of subject areas as the national curriculum but modified in content and objectives; and

6. a curriculum with specific social and personal development objectives for children with severe and complex physical, sensory and learning disabilities.

The different relationships to the national core curriculum represent an increasing need for specialised curriculum development and teaching. The following paragraphs give a brief description of each level of intervention and of the nature and degree of the resources likely to be needed.

1. *Technical Support to Follow a National Core Curriculum*

This level of intervention assumes that the individuals have the ability to follow the same curriculum as their contemporaries given appropriate technical assistance. It may be most appropriate for pupils with physical and sensory disabilities whose abilities to learn are not seriously impaired but who require special forms of access to the material to be learned. Assistance would take the form of making the material and activities in the teaching programme accessible according to the learner's disability. It may involve interpretation, the provision of special equipment and minor modifications of the learning environment.

The kinds of resource which might be required are:

- consultant support by teachers with appropriate specialist qualifications;
- the preparation and regular supply of learning materials modified for particular disabilities;
- interpretation for pupils with hearing impairment;
- non-teaching assistance;
- the provision and servicing of technical equipment; and
- in-service education for the primary and secondary teachers responsible for teaching the pupils concerned.

Special education expertise is clearly required for overall supervision and in particular for the first three types. The time required from specialist teachers to deliver consultant support to particular schools or classes should be a finite on-going commitment which can be calculated for a particular number of sessions for children and visits to schools.

The time requirements for other personnel such as interpreters, technicians and non-teaching assistants may represent a long-term commitment in some cases and a finite time in others. They should be specified during assessment and while setting up the arrangements for a particular pupil. Equipment and teaching materials will be other major resource elements.

The disabilities which give rise to special educational needs, for which such technical support might be appropriate, are those which are relatively uncomplicated and which have a low incidence. It is generally uneconomic to provide a full secondary curriculum in small special schools and difficult to do so in larger residential schools without very close cooperation with local secondary schools. This form of intervention is therefore most likely to be educationally and cost effective in primary and secondary schools.

2. Supplementary Teaching for the National Core Curriculum

This form of intervention is intended to facilitate an individual's access to the curriculum offered to other children of the same age. It will by definition involve additional teaching time. The two most common alternatives are:

- additional general teaching time to allow the class or subject teacher to give children with special educational needs extra tuition; or
- special education teacher time, appropriate to the individual's needs, to give supplementary special teaching in the regular class or elsewhere.

The resources involved in this type of intervention, in addition to many listed on p. 55, are:

- additional primary or secondary teaching hours; and
- special education teacher hours.

The nature of support teaching and the many variants in existence will be discussed later. Some issues have been recently investigated by Jean Garnett[1]. At this point it is important to note that the special education teacher's contribution can take one of the following forms:

- supplementary teaching of curriculum subjects; or
- specialist teaching such as linguistic skills in the case of children with hearing impairment.

The contribution can be made in the regular class, individually or in small groups withdrawn from the regular class and elsewhere. Both primary and secondary school teachers and special education teachers will also need to set aside a number of hours for planning and programme preparation.

3. Selective Involvement in the National Core Curriculum

The assumption here is that special education teachers and primary and secondary teachers will work together to develop a programme for individuals. This would involve working from a special education base and introducing and supporting individuals in regular classes for selected subjects and activities. With this type of intervention primary responsibility for the children's education might shift from being solely that of the regular class teacher to being a shared responsibility with the special education teacher.

The kinds of resource required for this kind of intervention are:

- special education teacher hours;
- non-teaching assistant hours;
- equipment and materials; and
- an appropriate special educational environment.

Special education teaching hours will have to cover teaching the group in special education base and support teaching in regular classes. In some instances non-teaching assistant time may also be necessary either to assist the special education teacher in the base or to support children in regular classes.

4. Selective Involvement in other Curriculum Activities

There is always likely to be a division between core elements of the national curriculum and the other curriculum activities that schools make available. The latter are less likely to be influenced by objective testing and pressure to achieve national standards. They may provide greater opportunities for children with special educational needs to learn with their contemporaries. The involvement, and the kinds of resource required will be similar in nature to (3) above.

5. A Modified Curriculum

The definition of a modified curriculum will become clearer in the light of national curriculum guidelines. It should imply that children with special educational needs are offered the same range of areas of experiences or subjects as other children but that the materials and learning objectives are significantly modified to take account of learning difficulties of all kinds. Children with moderate degrees of learning difficulty exist in significant numbers in primary and secondary schools as well as in special schools. This degree of curriculum modification will have relevance for a section of the school population which spans primary, secondary and special education. There will be a borderline, requiring definition, between variations that are acceptable within the core curriculum and the degree of modification necessary for children with moderate degrees of learning difficulty. As with other borderlines this will shift as schools become more or less able to teach the range of children who attend them.

Where provision is made in special classes or schools the kinds of resources required by this form of intervention are:

- subject teacher hours to prepare material;
- special education teacher hours;
- non-teaching assistant hours; and
- equipment and materials.

This degree of intervention would imply full-time special education teaching with teacher/pupil ratios more favourable than are general in primary and secondary schools in the area. In secondary schools it would be expected that specialist subject teachers should share, with special education teachers, responsibility for the modified teaching of their subjects. This commitment should be specified in terms of hours per term if the modified curriculum is to maintain quality of content and material as well as quality of methodology.

6. A Separate Curriculum

This form of curriculum, focusing on more limited objectives, is assumed to be appropriate for children with very severe and complex learning difficulties. Interaction with contemporaries is assumed to be limited and confined to social interaction. Shared educational experiences are less likely. Delivering a curriculum of this kind involves full-time special education teaching in modified environments. These are currently most often provided in special schools. It is important that special education teaching hours not only cover classroom work but also planning and supported social integration.

The resources involved are:

- special education teacher hours;
- non-teaching assistant hours;
- equipment and materials; and
- modified environment.

Summary

The descriptions of different degrees of curriculum variation and the resources involved are, it must be stressed, illustrative. There are alternatives but planning and communication would be facilitated by a general agreement along the lines proposed.

The Contact Type Dimension

The type of contact which a special education teacher has with children with special educational needs will vary. It will depend on the distance of the special education teacher from the child and whether contact is direct or indirect. The range may be from working with and through primary and secondary teachers to full responsibility for teaching a child. The nature and degree of that variation may be described as follows:

1. the supply of appropriate curriculum material;
2. distant consultation and specialist support;
3. distance special education teaching;
4. collaborative special education teaching;
5. supplementary special education teaching; and
6. full-time special education teaching.

Each of the different kinds and degrees of contact has implications for the use of time and for teacher preparation. As with the curriculum dimension there is a step by step move away from support for the regular teacher to separate provision. Brief descriptions of each step follow.

1. The Supply of Appropriate Curriculum Material

This form of intervention places the special education teacher at a distance from children with special educational needs. It assumes that the class or subject teacher is an effective manager of individual learning programmes but has insufficient time and knowledge to develop programmes and materials for individual children with special educational needs. The task of the special education service is to see that the regular teacher is supported and supplied with appropriate materials. Such provision may be most appropriate in primary schools.

The kinds of resources required are likely to be:

• special education teacher time;
• technician time to prepare materials for distribution; and
• administrative time to manage distribution.

The special education teacher time will be required to prepare materials for learning, to prepare school situations for using prepared materials and to supervise their use and effectiveness. Time calculations will have to differentiate between that required for setting up arrangements and that required to maintain them.

2. Distant Consultative Specialist Support

This contact involves making available experienced special education teachers to work with teachers in primary and secondary schools who have children with disabilities and special educational needs in their classes. It envisages that special education teachers, with appropriate expertise, will be available for consultation and advice, for programme planning and for authorising the supply of specialist equipment and material. It does not include the direct teaching of children with special educational needs.

The resource requirements are likely to be:

- special education teacher time;
- back up secretarial help to free teacher time; and
- materials and specialist equipment.

The total special education teacher time available will need to be sufficient to provide a range of knowledge and skills in teaching children with different disabilities. It may be an advantage if this form of service is linked to specialist provision in the area. It is unlikely that resources will be available to allocate a specific amount of time to each school in the area. This kind of provision may be most appropriate for children with less severe physical, sensory and specific learning disabilities. Time will be required to set up services and to gain the confidence of schools. Other commitments such as in-service education and maintenance time commitments need to be distinguished, in job descriptions, from work with schools and children.

3. Distance Special Education Teaching

This element is included in the continuum because new technology will make it increasingly practical as an answer to meeting special educational needs in local schools in sparsely populated areas. Using a radio or television network or video tapes the special education teacher can have regular interactive teaching sessions with pupils in their own schools or homes and set programmes to be managed by class and subject teachers between sessions.

The resource requirements are likely to be:

- special education teacher time;
- a radio or television teaching network;
- technician support; and
- administrative support.

The special education teacher time would be made up of development work with other teachers in the first instance together with direct distance teaching. These activities might also be carried out in conjunction with those set out in consultative support.

4. *Collaborative Special Education Teaching*

The essential features of this kind of provision are joint working arrangements between special education teachers and class and subject teachers in primary and secondary schools. A number of different terms are used to describe variations of the basic idea and different relationships between the teachers are implied by some of them.[2] Three variations may be distinguished for the purpose of this analysis. They are team teaching, co-teaching and support teaching.

In *team teaching* the special education teacher is a full- or part-time member of a team of teachers responsible for a group of children or an aspect of the curriculum. The special education teacher has responsibilities for making others in the team aware of special educational needs, working with them to develop teaching materials for such children within the team's overall programme and, where necessary, supporting individual children.

Co-teaching envisages a special education teacher working with a class or subject colleague to plan a teaching programme which takes into account the special needs of children in the class. It implies equal status and shared responsibility for the teaching programme with leadership and supporting roles alternating between the two teachers.

Support teaching is a term used in a variety of ways which sometimes includes co-teaching. In this analysis support teaching does not involve any responsibility for the overall subject or class teaching programme. It is used to describe the situation where a special education teacher works in regular classes to help individual children or small groups. The teaching programme will be set by the class or subject teacher and the specialist will be helping the individuals who have difficulties to make a better response to it. Of course active and tactful support teaching also helps to influence the class or subject teacher's programme as a whole.

The resource requirements will vary according to the variety of collaborative teaching planned but will include:

- special education teaching time; and
- liaison and planning time for special education and class or subject teachers.

This will often be one element in the work of a special education teacher. To be successful this kind of work involves close knowledge of schools and is usually most time effective when the special education teacher is on the staff of a primary or secondary school and when adequate time is set aside for planning.

5. Supplementary Special Education Teaching

The distinction made here between collaborative and supplementary teaching is that between additional help within the regular class and additional help given to individuals withdrawn from classes. The latter may be necessary, for example, to teach specific study skills to children with severe visual impairments, to improve the language skill of those with hearing impairments and to help children with emotional and behaviour difficulties.

The resource implications of this form of provision may include:

- special education teaching time;
- non-teaching assistant time;
- an appropriate base in which to work; and
- special materials and equipment.

The time requirements include both direct part-time teaching and liaison work with class and subject teachers. They may also include time to prepare work for management by class and subject teachers between direct teaching sessions.

6. Direct Specialist Teaching

This may be full- or part-time and within a special school or primary or secondary school. It assumes major responsibility for a child's programme but not necessarily teaching the whole of it.

The resource implications are:

- special education teaching time;
- non-teaching assistant time;
- an appropriate teaching base; and
- special materials and equipment.

In addition to time allocated to direct teaching, teachers and non-teaching assistants will require an allocation of time for liaison and to support individuals in regular classes.

The Time Intensity Dimension

Although the contact type dimension has time implications, special educational interventions can vary both in the intensity of their time demands each day or week and the length of time that a particular time commitment may be necessary. It may be helpful to specify a time component in assessment if resource requirements are to be known. Possible points on a continuum might be:

1. intermittent support on demand;
2. regular support;
3. regular additional teaching;
4. part-time special education;
5. full-time day special education; and
6. residential special education.

One of the important aspects of breaking down activities with more precision is to have time commitments to children with special educational needs and from their teachers expressed in the same terms.

When considering the time implications of different levels of work it is necessary to consider other kinds of time commitment. Time allowances for them are not always made clear in job descriptions. Four are additional to the contact time involved in the 'time intensity' dimension. These are:

- Initiation Time. This is the time required to set up a particular service. In may involve considerable effort to explain arrangements and to prepare teachers for them.
- Maintenance Time. Once established services require maintenance time, that is time to review and discuss arrangements with school staffs, to ensure their continued effectiveness.
- Context Change Time. Under this heading would come various forms of consultation and in-service education aimed to improve the ability of schools and teachers to manage learning and to reduce the number of special educational needs which may arise. Activity may be school based or elsewhere. It should be a cooperative activity with other professionals who work with schools and not isolated from other initiatives.
- Special Educational Preparation Time. The time required to prepare materials and individual programmes can be considerable at certain times in the development of support teaching services and this needs to be allocated.

1. Intermittent Support

This is the least commitment of time to individual children on the continuum. At a result of assessment a child's needs are known, the potential to meet them within a primary or secondary school is available and is expected to be adequate. The ready availability of consultant support will enable a child's teacher and school to deal with assessed needs with confidence. The time commitment will not be predictable and will depend on the effectiveness of initiation and maintenance arrangements. It might amount to one or two supervision sessions per year.

2. Regular Support

Although the phrase is capable of many interpretations, it is used here to indicate that the individual child will get regular visits on a planned basis. Those teaching the child can count on that regular commitment to provide support and to evaluate progress a specific number of times each term.

3. Regular Teaching Sessions

This level of intervention is associated with direct teaching by a special educator. It is expected that the number of teaching sessions a child needs will be specified. It is assumed that they will be at least weekly and may be individual or in small groups.

4. Part-time Special Education

This description is intended to cover education in special classes wherever they are. The number of sessions each week, which are required in individual cases, will vary but for a defined period it should be possible to specify the number to be spent in a regular classroom and in a special group.

5. Day Special Education

This time commitment will cover the special school day and the hours that teachers are involved in its work.

6. Residential Special Education

The commitment of time will be greatest in the boarding school where teachers may be involved in the lives of the children for more than the normal school day.

While the last three of the elements of the range are traditional and relatively easy to quantify in terms of teacher time, the first two are often offered without any real idea of what is possible. As a result expectations may be too high and conscientious teachers may be under additional stress. The aim is to specify time commitments to children and to match them to the time constraints, situations and patterns of work of individual teachers.

The Environment Dimension

One of the aspects of special education identified in the Warnock Report was an appropriate environment. While much attention has been devoted to the issue of integration, the actual nature of environmental variation which exists or might be necessary has seldom been specified. There will be variations that are necessary because of different disabilities, such as a proper acoustic environment for those with hearing impairments, an accessible environment for those with mobility problems and an appropriate environment for educating children with emotional difficulties. Some modifications, such as carpeting in primary and secondary schools, may help all children and teachers and, by reducing noise, diminish the incidence of behaviour difficulties. What is suggested here is that, in addition to special features, there is a continuum expressed in terms of increasing variation from the general environment in primary and secondary schools. The continuum implies an increasing degree of speciality and distance from the environments in which the majority of children are educated in the authority area.

1. the environment of the regular classroom;
2. a combination of the regular classroom environment and a special setting within a primary or secondary school;
3. a combination of the regular classroom and special setting outside a primary or secondary school;
4. a special setting inside a primary or secondary school such as a unit or special class;
5. a special setting outside a primary or secondary school such as a day special unit or school; and
6. a special residential setting.

It is important to visualise these environmental variations as responses to children's needs. They should be kept constantly under review. At present they tend to be considered simply as a range of alternative placements.

Comment

The dimensions set out are among the most common. They are not always specified in detail or related one to another. There are other dimensions which may be equally important for the quality of provision which are discussed in the next two chapters.

Notes

1. J. Garnett, 'Support teaching: taking a closer look', *British Journal of Special Education*, Vol. 15, No. 1, March 1988.
2. As above.

CHAPTER 6

Further Dimensions

The previous chapter looked at the most common aspects of special education. Other dimensions also help to define what is happening when special education is being provided. In this chapter the dimensions of technology, specialist knowledge, teacher skills, parental involvement and relationships, together with the contribution of other educational professionals, are described.

The Relationship Dimension

Although most often thought of in connection with children with emotional and behaviour disorders, relationships are very important in the education of all children with special educational needs. The arguments for and against integration have to be seen in terms of enabling children with disabilities and significant difficulties to develop relationships with their contemporaries. The case for integration is not just a consequence of relative definitions and higher expectations. It is primarily based on the assumption that as adults these children are now expected to live and function in the same neighbourhood as their contemporaries when they leave school. Completely separate special education, however severe the need, is a very inadequate preparation for life in the community. Nevertheless during the period of schooling decisions will have to be made about the degree of association which may be most beneficial for the individual.

There is some evidence to suggest that activities and relationships between children with disabilities and others do not always arise spontaneously and that adult encouragement and management may be necessary. A policy of integration, or more properly of preparation for adulthood, requires an active approach to developing the friendships and social skills of children with special educational needs. Assessment should indicate how relationship needs might be met within individual programmes. The continuum might range from unplanned association to carefully planned individual contacts.

The different levels from which to choose might be:

1.   unplanned free association in the regular school;
2/3. planned association in the regular school;
4/5. planned and managed regular interaction on a group basis; and
6.   planned and managed limited interaction on an individual basis.

The association and interaction outlined is as necessary for children without disabilities and difficulties as for those with them. Their understanding of, and relationships with, contemporaries who are disabled will be a significant element in the development of positive attitudes and in the success of subsequent community care and participation programmes. Both depend on overcoming fears and misunderstandings, which are not confined to one group, during school life.

1. Unplanned Free Association in the Regular School

In this case it is assumed that a disabled child or a child with special educational needs has adequate and appropriate social relationships with other children. No particular planning or programme is necessary to ensure healthy social development.

2/3. Planned Association in the Regular School

This may occur most often when individuals join regular classes from units or special classes in the same school. It is included as a reminder that the social relationship aspects of integrative educational arrangements needs as much attention as the more obvious educational aspects.

4/5. Planned and Managed Regular Interaction

This can be done in a number of ways. One method involves special and regular classes in a school having a number of weeks of shared educational activities in each school year. Another involves pairs of classes having periods each week with a team of teachers. It is, of course, more difficult but not impossible, to arrange between separate special schools and primary and secondary schools. There is evidence of an increasing amount of such activity[1] and it is facilitated when specific time is allotted to fostering such interaction.

6. Planned and Managed Limited Interaction

This can take a number of forms but perhaps the most common is the 'buddy' approach, where children with special educational needs share regular periods with a non-disabled child. Educational or social activities are planned which both can share. To be effective time for such contacts have to be built into the allocation of teacher and non-teaching assistant time.

The Dimension of Technology

This dimension is increasing in importance with every new application of micro-electronics to the field of disability. It includes not only applications which enhance control over the environment but also those which aid communication and which facilitate the access to and management of information. There are an increasing number of technological means of decreasing the handicapping effects of disabilities and significant difficulties. The different levels which are outlined are tentative but indicate one way of marking off the continuum.

1. accessibility to the technology which is normally available in the regular classroom;
2. simple personal aids to vision, hearing, fine movement and mobility together with access to the technology normally available in the regular classroom;
3. special personal equipment such as electronic mobility aids and complex communication aids, specialised means of access to equipment and material;
4. integrated and complex personal means of environmental control, mobility and access to information in the regular environment; and
5. a special electronically managed and accessible environment for living and learning.

The implications of the increased use of technology are enormous. Not only will personal equipment make regular environments less handicapping but the children will have greater direct access to learning materials of all kinds. Teachers will need to be able to manage the learning rather than be the means by which information is transmitted to children. There will be a requirement for personnel to develop, service and maintain equipment. In the long run education services will need to develop electronic information and mail networks to enable students who are disabled to communicate with their teachers and with each other.

The Dimension of Knowledge

It is possible to recognise a variety of different combinations of the knowledge necessary for recognition as a special education teacher. The approach to special education outlined in Chapter 3 implies that special education teacher training will be built on the initial training and qualification of primary and secondary teachers. Assumptions then have to be made about the training of primary and secondary teachers as a basis on which this knowledge is built. The combinations which follow have been chosen because they reflect the incidence of different special educational needs and their associated disabilities.

1. knowledge of the commoner learning and behaviour difficulties which occur in primary and secondary schools;
2. knowledge of the educational need associated with the commoner physical and sensory disabilities found in primary and secondary schools;
3. specific knowledge about behaviour difficulties, moderate learning difficulties and specific learning difficulties;
4. specific knowledge about severe degrees of sensory and physical disabilities and severe learning difficulties;
5. specific knowledge of multiple and profound disabilities and learning difficulties; and
6. leadership, management and evaluation skills in special education.

A hierarchical element may be evident but is not necessary to the analysis. There are, however, training and deployment implications of such a continuum. As a result of assessing both children and the teaching force available it may become possible to decide where best a particular kind and degree of knowledge is necessary and best deployed.

The Dimension of Skills

Although closely related to knowledge, the skills dimension has been isolated to make a particular point about provision. For example the skills of finger spelling and using braille are very specific and can be made available by a number of different people in addition to special education teachers. This is a dimension where some overlap with the work of primary and secondary teachers can be taken into account. It will also have relevance to the training and work of non-teaching assistants. One way of discriminating the range of skill might be as follows:

1. minor special education skills, which it is hoped that all primary and secondary school teachers will eventually acquire through initial or in-service training, that are necessary to meet the wide range of minor special educational needs;
2/3. general special education skills sufficient to enable special education teachers in primary and secondary schools adequately to meet needs that are not so great as to require that a statement be made;
4. common disability-specific skills;
5. minority disability-specific skills; and
6. complex combinations of disability-specific skills.

The descriptions of the skill levels which follow are tentative and do not include management, leadership and evaluation skills. While skills are closely linked with knowledge there is also value in making a distinction between the range of skills a person has and the level of skill necessary for work in particular situations, with children with different degrees of special educational need and in different patterns of organisation.

1. Minor Special Education Skills

The skills at this level are currently made available by a range of special education personnel but they are increasingly to be found in the work of primary and secondary school teachers. A possible array of skills at this level is listed below:

- ability to recognise that a special educational need exists;
- the presentation of factual data to describe the problem;
- knowing when to seek further help and from whom;
- ability to initiate and use simple assessment procedures;
- ability to initiate and use simple special programmes; and
- ability to evaluate the effects of simple programmes.

These skills assume that all trained teachers will have a basic level of competence in programme planning and record keeping. Record keeping is envisaged here as a basis for teaching: the teacher will know the objectives of teaching, what has been accomplished by each child and the general learning characteristics of individual pupils. At present much special education teacher time is taken up with gathering information about children which ought to be regularly recorded and brought together before consultation.

2/3. General Special Education Skills

These skills are those expected of special education teachers on the staff of, or working regularly with, primary and secondary schools. It is assumed that these teachers will have experience of and be familiar with the work of such schools. It is also assumed that there will be a leadership structure within which their work is managed. The skills are those necessary to meet the range of special educational needs that commonly arise in schools and which do not normally require a statement to be made before they can be met. They include:

- the assessment of children with common learning and behaviour difficulties;
- the ability to recognise and give general advice about less severe physical and sensory disabilities;
- knowing when to seek further help and from whom;
- programme planning, jointly with other teachers and parents, for individual children and small groups;
- ability to teach with other teachers in a team, in collaboration and in a supporting capacity; and
- skills in team working with other professionals.

In addition to general teaching competence it is clear that the skills of working with others are crucial to success. It is also important that special education teachers working within schools need to know and feel part of the special education service as a whole.

4. Common Disability-specific Skills

These skills are envisaged as special proficiencies which are built on general special education skills. The teacher becomes experienced in working with children with more marked degrees of special educational need of a particular type such as moderate learning difficulties. The range might include:

- skills involved in managing emotional and behaviour difficulties; and
- skills appropriate for teaching children with moderate learning difficulties.

The list is not exhaustive but illustrative and the borderline between this group of skills and those in the next group is far from clear. It is, however, necessary to make some distinctions in order to match training provision and demand.

5. Minority Disability-specific Skills

This level of skill is seen as related to specific disabilities, such as impairments of vision and hearing, with relatively small incidences. The range might include:

• reading and writing braille;
• various forms of oral and manual communication, signing and finger spelling; and
• skills involved in teaching children with specific learning difficulties.

Again the list is illustrative. It is assumed that this level will involve proficiency-specific skills necessary to teach children with marked but relatively uncomplicated disabilities, whereas the next level would involve a greater complexity of needs.

6. Complex Combinations of Disability-specific Skills

At this level we would assume a very highly skilled and trained person able to work with children with profound and multiple disabilities and with the help of assistants to devise and carry out complex educational and training procedures.

Not included on this continuum, but of great importance, are managerial and leadership skills. These are necessary in many forms of special education and are vital to effective special education services.

The Supporting Education Service Professional Dimension

This dimension is intended to describe the different kinds of intervention made by other professionals employed in the education service. It primarily covers the contributions of educational psychologists and educational social workers. It is important to stress that this dimension relates solely to the contribution made to the provision of special education through support and consultation and more rarely through work with children. It is not intended to cover vital aspects of work such as assessment, setting up arrangements and their review and evaluation. It might also cover the work of some peripatetic and advisory teachers. The dimension is seen in terms of the time contract made with an individual child, an individual teacher or a school after assessment to deliver special education. The different levels of intervention might be as follows:

1. available for advice and support;
2. a regular review of a child's progress or of provision;
3. regular visits once per term for up to a session;

4. regular visits once per month for up to a session;
5. regular visits once per week for up to a session; and
6. daily visits.

The time element will of course determine what can be done. It is unlikely that for example that daily visits will be possible for more than a brief period.

1. *Available for Advice and Support*

It is all too easy for individuals to be drawn into major time commitments on the grounds of providing a service. However, individual demands result in a very uneven distribution of effort. This level of intervention is intended to cover very sporadic and general maintenance activities.

Although the most common description of service availability, it is the most difficult to analyse and quantify. It has to be assumed that the time available to each school will be less than one half-session each term. For the time to be used effectively, setting up time has to have been spent in schools to establish trust and to establish the limits of what the service is able to do. Given that this has been done, the amount of time to be allocated to this level of service is, in practice, probably what can be spared once contractual arrangements have been made.

2. *A Regular Review*

Again there will be a difference between making an assessment of need during a first visit to a school and making one when relationships have been established. Elements in such a visit or visits would normally include:

- an interview with the headteacher;
- an interview with the class teacher;
- an interview with the child;
- an interview with the parents; and
- discussions of the results and possible actions.

It is assumed that this level of intervention will not occur more than once or twice a year. Allowing a minimum of an hour for each of these activities the total time would be five hours; research has indicated that for educational psychologists eight hours would in some cases not be unreasonable. Major reductions in the time taken are possible if the school has good records and good relationships with parents. They are also possible if the school produces a coherent written report describing the problem, the actions taken and the results of those actions. Much depends on the starting point for visiting professionals.

3. Regular Termly Visits

Once these are established as a working practice it becomes possible to look at the use of time. The visits would be part of provision only when they enabled the staff of schools to work more effectively with children already identified to have needs. Activities during visits might include:

- discussion of children needing reassessment;
- discussion of the progress of children receiving special education;
- discussion of school special educational developments including assessment and recording, forms of provision and evaluation. In the case of educational social workers it would include relationships with parents etc.

Only where the last two are concerned with children with known needs could these activities be seen as provision. In summary this degree of intervention would mainly be of a maintenance nature ensuring that the use of more time-intensive interventions were minimised.

4. Regular Monthly Visits

To the activities outlined as termly could be added some contact with individual children. A relatively brief monthly interview with the teacher and or the child may be sufficient in some circumstances to maintain morale and progress. It is important that this is planned positively and that it is what is *needed* rather than what is *possible*.

5. Regular Weekly Visits

The activities which could be undertaken with this time commitment might include:

- regular sessions with individual children or small groups;
- regular support work and teaching in the classroom;
- regular work with parents;
- a sessional school-based in-service training programme; and
- a school-based research programme.

This is the intervention level at which shared teaching might occur.

6. Daily Visits

Except in the case of a shared teacher this degree of intervention is a major commitment of resources and should therefore be either very short-term or confined to very complex problems. The activities would be similar to those described in (5) above.

Parental Dimensions

There are two interrelated parental dimensions of special education: parental involvement in a child's problem and parental participation in a child's education. The first of these is more evident where there are emotional and behaviour difficulties but may be an important element in fostering the growth, development and learning of any child with special educational needs within the family, particularly during adolescence. The second is systematic development of the idea of partnership.

Parental Involvement

This dimension describes parental needs which may be determined during assessment. Some parents may require intensive counselling and personal help to work positively with their children. Many of the issues associated with involvement become particularly evident in the pre-school years or during adolescence and transition to adult and working life, but they are, however, crucial throughout a child's education. Possible points on a continuum might be:

1. parents need good average home–school relationships;
2. parents require above average home–school relationships;
3. parents require termly counselling sessions;
4. parents require monthly counselling sessions;
5. parents require weekly counselling sessions; and
6. parents require intensive family casework.

Again the idea is to indicate a range which may be varied locally. Special educators will recognise how much some children's progress depends on providing appropriate help for parents when they are very involved in their children's disabilities and difficulties.

Parental Participation

The provision of special education is increasingly involving parents. Home teaching programmes for young children, shared reading programmes for older children and the use of home–school diaries are examples of active parental involvement on a regular basis. This aspect of parental involvement is defined separately from the family and social aspect and is described here because it is clearly a significant component of effective special education. There are two distinct ways in which the contribution can be made: in relation to the parent's own child, usually at home; and in helping teachers in schools with particular activities. The different levels might be:

- no planned involvement;
- regular termly interchange of information;
- spending regular weekly sessions in school or keeping a weekly home–school diary;
- keeping a daily home–school diary;
- planned teaching at home to supplement a school's programme; and
- daily home teaching sessions following a programme.

The first of these levels is included to cover situations where, perhaps for the time being, parental involvement in a child's education may be undesirable or indeed counterproductive, as in the case of some emotional and behaviour difficulties.

Comment

The dimensions outlined in this chapter complete those for which the local education authority and its employees may be directly responsible. There are others, to be discussed in the next chapter, that involve other services and which in the terms of the 1981 Act the local education authority cannot easily provide on its own.

Note

1. S. Jowett, S. Hegarty and D. Moses, *Joining Forces: A Study of Links between Ordinary and Special Schools*, NFER/Nelson, 1988.

CHAPTER 7

Other Professional Contributions

Good special educational provision has always been associated with multiprofessional approaches to helping children and young people with disabilities and significant difficulties. Current legislation separates educational responsibilities from those of health and social services and makes it difficult to ensure that a child gets contributions from these services as part of a coordinated programme.

The parameters or dimensions which are an educational responsibility have now been outlined. It is suggested that the same approach could be adopted by social service departments and district health authorities to describe their contributions. The following sections suggest dimensions and levels of intervention for those services.

It is assumed that health and social services are likely to require some structure for their contributions, but the examples are not intended to suggest how they might be made. They illustrate a comparable structure which might help communication within multiprofessional teams.

Health Service Dimensions

For the purposes of this discussion two dimensions have been identified:

1. medical and nursing care; and
2. treatment and therapy.

In both cases it should be possible for the health service contribution to assessment to include an indication of the nature and degree of intervention that is necessary as well as what is possible. A clearer definition of levels of need and provision may provide a better basis for service delivery.

Medical and Nursing Oversight and Care

Medical and nursing care has always been a significant element in special education. Although it has become less dominant in determining the nature of provision, it is still a vital component of some provision. This dimension, it is assumed, will range from the medical and nursing care that is considered necessary for all children to the sustained care necessary for children with particular health problems from which special educational needs might arise. Levels of intervention might be:

1. That available for all other children. This might involve the primary health care team, including the general practitioner, and the school health services available in the area.
2. A health service contribution to programme planning. This level of intervention is assumed to involve the district child development team making a contribution to assessment and to decisions about the nature of an individual's special education programme.
3. A regular review of health care. This step on a continuum might involve medical and nursing oversight and, in particular, a review at regular intervals by either the primary health care or the district child development teams.
4. Regular treatment sessions. For children with some conditions, giving rise to special educational needs, regular treatment may be necessary.
5. Daily medical and nursing care. This level of intervention might be appropriate in day special schools. It assumes the continued existence of separate special provision for children with physical disabilities and conditions.
6. 24-hour medical and nursing care. This level of oversight may be necessary in some residential special schools and will also be evident when children are educated while in hospital.

Health authorities and health service professionals will naturally determine the nature and level of what is to be provided. However, information in this form may be helpful to education authorities when making decisions about where to provide for individual children.

Therapy

Speech, occupational and physio-therapy are often essential elements in a special education programme. They are provided by health authorities. Each district authority and each profession will determine its own priorities but again it should be possible during assessment to arrive at an indication of levels of intervention necessary and possible. The suggested levels might be:

1. No therapy appropriate or necessary. This is an obvious starting point on the continuum where the child's special educational needs do not include associated therapies provided by health authorities.
2. A consultant contribution to the programme. Here it is assumed that therapists will not only contribute to assessment but will also indicate, where necessary, what might be included in an individual programme other than their direct work with children;
3. A regular review of progress. It is increasingly evident that a shortage of therapists is making it necessary to work with and through others. This level of intervention implies that the therapist will see an individual at intervals between which parents and teachers will carry out activities suggested by therapists within their own programmes.
4. Regular therapy sessions. This is the first level where it is suggested that direct regular contact with the child with special educational needs might take place. The timing of sessions and intervals between them is a matter for the therapists concerned.
5. Weekly therapy sessions.
6. Daily therapy sessions.

The last two points on the continuum are relatively obvious examples of current practices.

Social Service Dimensions

There are a number of areas of work where education and social services have common interests. Three in particular should be noted with respect to special education. They are:

- Provision and services for children under five. Early intervention programmes for young children with special educational needs are important. Their place within a context of educational, social service and voluntary organisation provision is often uncertain.
- The borderline between provision for children of school age with emotional and behaviour difficulties, for which education authorities

are responsible, and provision for children and young people with acute social difficulties and delinquency, for which social services are responsible.

• Post-school provision for young people with disabilities is also an area where the two services have common concerns.

Many of the children and young people for whom social services have responsibilities also have special educational needs and close cooperation between both services is vital. Social services can make significant contributions to the assessment of special educational needs and may also contribute to meeting them.

The service already has a framework of levels of training and levels of work which is, in many ways, consistent with what is being advocated for special education. However, the service may have different priorities with greater emphasis on case work with children, young people and their families than on education. Where arrangements to meet special educational needs are concerned there might be two dimensions relating to the social service status of the child and family and the actions being taken by social workers.

The Social Service Status Dimension

This is intended to denote the degree to which the child and the family are a concern of social services. It might range from no knowledge of, and involvement with, a family through various forms of child care to 24-hour residential care.

The existence of disabilities and special educational needs is quite independent of social service status. Nevertheless the local education authority's duties have to be exercised with due concern for such a status. Similarly, the social service department needs to work closely with education authorities where special educational needs exist and a child is the subject of a statement. The department will have 'parental' rights and duties in the process of making a statement. A recognition of each other's responsibilities and levels of service delivery is important.

One approach to the different levels of social service intervention is suggested. This is:

1. the child and family are not known to the service;
2. the family is 'known' but there is no current work going on with the child or family;
3. the child is the subject of a supervision order;
4. the child is in care and fostered;
5. the child is in care and in children's home or boarding school; and
6. the child is in a closed or special institution.

Again it is important to recognise that these are suggestions and that the services themselves will have their own levels of work. Within a local authority area it will be helpful if there is discussion about the relationships between the levels of work of each department and the means of making them compatible.

Social Service Involvement

In addition to the status of the child and family there may be different levels of work by social service professionals with children and families. This may range from no current action through periodic visits to intensive family case work. A suggested continuum with levels of intervention work might be:

1. no current activities;
2. support for the child and family is available on request;
3. periodic visits are made to the home;
4. regular supervision and review of the child's needs and the family situation;
5. regular family case work; and
6. intensive family therapy.

This rough attempt to define levels of work rather than levels of need may also serve as a basis for allocating professional time. However, the main purpose of giving an indication is to show how communication could improve by a more precise statement of need and involvement.

Special Education and Other Services

These dimensions are an attempt to recognise the multiprofessional nature of appropriate provision for children with severe and complex disabilities which may involve health service contributions and social service relationships with families. The 1981 Act, while promoting multiprofessional assessment, has made multiprofessional provision much harder to achieve.

What the education authority is to provide, as set out in a statement, is a form of contract with the parents. The education authority may be legally vulnerable if the specified arrangements are not made. However, aspects of special educational needs which can be met only by provision made by other services are not guaranteed. There appears no way in which children and their parents can be assured of a comprehensive programme involving health, social service and educational elements.

The problem can only be noted in this context. The main aim is to help those in the education and associated services to be clearer about the nature of special education and the means of delivering it in whatever form of pre-school, primary, secondary and further education provision is made in an area.

CHAPTER 8

Why Dimensions and Levels

Introduction

A descriptive system of different dimensions and levels has been outlined based on the assumption that special education is a variation of the education provided nationally and locally for all children. The need for such a framework has been argued on the basis of the inadequacy of current definitions. It may now be helpful to look at the framework as a whole.

It must be emphasised that the framework is illustrative. In practice the dimensions, like the curriculum framework, should be negotiable. It might be desirable to have agreement at a national level. A next stage might be for academic and service-providing specialists to refine and evaluate what at this stage is a sketch. It is assumed that levels of intervention will be determined empirically by each local education authority as a result of planning an integrated special education service within available resources.

Special Education as a Changing Variation

The framework described is a relative one. Its dimensions and levels are relative to existing primary and secondary school practices. The proposition is that what constitutes special education is not fixed. The nature of special educational needs and the provision to meet them will vary over time with variations in the objectives and effectiveness of primary and secondary education.

One of the major problems of developing a conceptual framework for the delivery of special education is to relate it to the dynamics of the growth and development of schools. It is necessary to take into account all the theoretical and practical issues currently being debated within compulsory education.

The borderline between regular and special educational arrangements is bound to vary from school to school and from authority to authority. Among the factors which influence this variation are:

- the intentions of government and their interpretation by different education authorities and schools;
- the intentions of education authorities with respect to the schools in their areas;
- the intentions of individual schools as expressed in their objectives and curricula;
- the differences between schools in their implementation of national, local education authority and their own intentions and their responsiveness to individual differences;
- the current developmental state of a school in respect of its dynamic processes of self-evaluation and curriculum development;
- the learning objectives set by teachers either as members of a school staff working to agreed ends or as individuals.

Attention to curriculum development within individual schools and to improving a school's responsiveness to individual needs is important. It is necessary to recognise that each primary or secondary school, as well as each special school and supporting service, will be at a different stage of development with respect to its objectives, curriculum, its working practices and corporate life. These variations will persist even within a nationally determined framework.

The dynamic processes of curriculum development in schools for children with moderate learning difficulties are currently the subject of study by a team at the London Institute of Education.[1,2,3] The conceptual framework being developed recognises that the extent and nature of individual needs is closely related to a school's perceptions of its functions, its internal communications network and the commitment of the staff to agreed objectives and procedures. There are important lessons from this project which are applicable to the way primary and secondary schools recognize and meet special educational needs and the changing borderline between general and special needs.

However, preoccupation with variations between schools should not lead to the neglect of service-delivery issues. The different stages of development of schools and authorities will only influence where the borderline between regular and special education is to be drawn at any one time. It will not influence the dimensions of the latter but it will have some effect on the levels of intervention that may be necessary. Any framework must take account of varying baselines between regular and special education in individual schools and local education authorities.

Special Education as a Necessary Variation

It is important to establish that special educational arrangements do not exist as of right. They exist because of needs that cannot, at a particular time, be met by average teachers with the average resources available. What is being provided is a practical response to needs which arise because regular education is not sufficiently flexible, knowledgeable and experienced to meet all the individual needs which may arise in a school population.

Because of human limitations it may never be possible to meet all such needs; but to attempt to do so should be an objective of any school or education system. This aspiration is essential if schools and education authorities are to minimise the number of special educational needs which may arise and if special education is to remain within the mainstream of education.

Without direction schools are prone to demand more and more special provision. Special education must, therefore, be described in terms which link it to primary and secondary education. Language which unnecessarily sharpens distinctions should be avoided.

This is not just a theoretical issue or a pious hope. It is an important aspect of resource management since special arrangements may cost more than regular ones. The relationship between regular and special provision is one where additional or different provision should be seen as a necessary, but interim, solution to overcome the current limitations of schools.

A second reason for avoiding unnecessary distinctions is a social one. The close links between regular and special education are an integral part of progress towards ensuring that young people with disabilities and difficulties and their contemporaries are educated to recognise each other as individuals. If those with special educational needs are to contribute as adults to the society in which they live, educators must seek the maximum common ground and interaction between primary, secondary and special education.

A Framework of Dimensions and Levels

It is suggested that a framework is essential for planning service delivery. While always being seen as interim, the timescale is likely to be one of

Table 8.1

Situational Dimensions				Educational
Levels	*Curriculum*	*Environment*	*Technology*	*Relationships*
I	Technical support for the national core curriculum	The regular classroom	Regular classroom technology	Unplanned free association in the regular school
II	Teaching to supplement the national core curriculum	Combination of regular classroom and special setting in primary and secondary school	Simple personal aids to vision, hearing and mobility Plus Level I provision	Daily planned association in the regular school
III	Selective involvement in national core curriculum	Combination of regular classroom and special setting outside primary and secondary school	Special personal equipment and specialised access to curriculum	
IV	Selective involvement in other curriculum activities	A special setting (unit or class) inside a primary or secondary school	Integrated and complex means of environmental control and access	Regular planned and managed group interaction
V	Modified national core curriculum teaching	A special setting outside a primary or secondary school	A specially electronically managed environment	
VI	A separate special curriculum	A special residential setting		Limited planned and managed individual interaction

Dimensions	Educational Dimensions				
Contact type	Knowledge	Skills	Time intensity	Time duration	Supporting professionals
The supply of appropriate curriculum material to class teacher	Commoner learning and behaviour difficulties	Minor special education skills	Intermittent support on demand	For half a term	Available for advice and support
Distance consultation and specialist support to class teacher	Needs associated with commoner physical and sensory disabilities	General special education skills	Regular support	For a team	Assessment visits
Distance special education teaching	Specific knowledge of moderate and specific learning and behaviour difficulties		Regular additional teaching	For a school year	Visits once a term
Collaborative special education teaching	Specific knowledge of severe sensory and learning disabilities	Common disability-specific skills	Part-time special education teaching	For the infant junior or secondary years	Visits once a month
Supplementary special education teaching	Knowledge of multiple and profound disabilities		Day special education	For school life	Weekly visits
Full-time special education teaching	Leadership, management and research knowledge	Complex specific multi-disability skills	Residential special education		Daily visits

Table 8.1 continued

	Shared Dimensions—Health Services	
Levels	Medical and nursing	Therapy
I	Available	None necessary
II	Contribution to programme	Consultant contribution to programme
III	Regular review health care	Regular review of progress
IV	Regular treatment sessions	Regular therapy sessions
V	Daily medical and nursing care	Weekly therapy sessions
VI	24-hour medical and nursing oversight	Daily therapy sessions

years rather than days. Its dimensions draw attention to the essential characteristics of provision and its levels indicate the extent to which regular provision has to be supplemented, adapted and altered to meet particular special educational needs.

The framework should enable administrators and professionals to describe what is being done. It should facilitate communication, make job descriptions easier to understand and enable those not in the special field to understand what is meant by special education. Above all it should challenge the assumptions currently made on the basis of descriptive indicators such as location, professional qualification and category of need.

If we set out all the dimensions and levels in the form of a table, (Table 8.1), it becomes possible to consider an individual's range of needs in terms of each dimension. We can draw a profile across the range of

Shared Dimensions—Social Services		Parental Contributions	
Child care status	*Social service involvement*	*Parental involvement*	*Parental participation*
None	None	Average home-school relationships	No planned involvement
Family 'known'	Support available	Very above average home-school relationships	Regular termly interchange of information
Supervision order	Periodic visits	Termly counselling sessions	Weekly sessions in school or weekly home-school diary
In care fostered	Regular supervision of family	Monthly counselling sessions	Keeping a daily home-school diary
In care children's home or boarding school	Regular family casework	Weekly counselling sessions	Planned teaching at home to supplement school programme
In closed or special institution	Intensive family therapy	Intensive family casework	Daily home teaching programme

dimensions from level to level in each. Similarly we can describe a location or service in terms of the profile of levels and dimensions which define what is being delivered.

Summary

Looking at the assessed needs of individual children it should be possible to determine at what point on each dimension some form of intervention would be most appropriate and to arrive at a profile of the levels of the provision to be made. Up to now a look at needs has been most often followed by the question 'where?' rather than 'what?' This analysis should lead to the ability to state more clearly what kinds of intervention on each dimension are recommended.

Similarly, there is no satisfactory way to describe the special education being provided in a particular location. The terms in current use relate to the disabilities and difficulties of the children rather than what is being provided for them. Using the dimensions and levels it should be possible to describe the characteristics of each form of special education without recourse to disability labels and locational stereotypes.

It should also be possible to define the dimensions and levels of intervention expected of teachers working in different special educational provision with the advantage of a better use of skills and time.

Other fields of professional training recognise levels of work and levels of training related to them. Social work is one example. One of the problems of special education teacher training has, for many years, been a lack of precision in this respect. The suggested framework may enable those responsible for training with the definition of the purposes of different courses.

Having broadly defined the uses of the framework the next chapter will look at these applications in more detail.

Notes

1. J. Ireson, P. Evans, P. Redmond, and K. Wedell, 'Developing the curriculum for children with learning difficulties: towards a grounded model', *British Education Research Journal* (in press).
2. J. Ireson, P. Evans, P. Redmond and K. Wedell, 'Comparing the curriculum development process in Special (MLD) schools: a systematic qualitative approach', *European Journal of Educational Research*, Vol. 3, pp. 147–60.
3. P. Evans, 'Towards a sociology of special education, in R. Bunden (ed.) *Successful Learning, Education and Child Psychology 5*. British Psychological Society, Leicester.

CHAPTER 9

Management and Resource Implications

Introduction

The question of variation in the baseline from which a framework of dimensions and levels is derived was outlined in the previous chapter. Its relationship to the internal processes of schools was also briefly discussed. In this chapter attention will turn to the positive advantages of such a framework.

The Advantages of a Framework

It is suggested that there are at least six compelling reasons for having a framework of the kind outlined. These are to:

- translate general assessment data about individuals into terms which describe more exactly the nature and degree of intervention necessary to meet their needs;
- describe with more precision the characteristics of different forms of special educational provision;
- describe the work of special education teachers, particularly those working in primary and secondary schools and in peripatetic and support teaching services, with greater accuracy;
- enable the detailed planning of special educational services and facilities to meet a defined range of dimensions and levels of need;
- enable the initial and in-service education for teachers and other personnel to be more precisely defined and planned with reference to

degrees of special educational needs and the levels of training necessary to meet them; and
• enable available resources to be used more effectively.

Each of the advantages is interrelated and the effects of using a framework of this type could be said to be cumulative. Each aspect will be discussed separately but is to some extent dependent on the others.

Translating Assessed Needs to Provision

Present procedures for assessment produce a considerable volume of information about individual children. The number of different professional perspectives represented may vary, but the cumulative effect is usually a comprehensive view of a child's assets and deficits.

For a variety of reasons assessed needs are rarely translated into specified forms of appropriate provision or intervention. It is true that some reasons for this are relate to limited resources or limited control over them. It is equally true that there are pressures to make recommendations match existing provision. The outcome, in most cases, depends on the answers to two relatively crude questions:

• Shall we make a statement of this child's special educational needs and the provision to be made to meet them?
• Where shall we place this child so that his or her needs can be met?

It is argued that difficulties in translating assessed need into necessary provision result from a lack of a descriptive system.

Provision and services for children whose needs are not considered sufficient to justify a statement are seldom specified. As a result the answer to the first question may be based on whether any provision is necessary at all. It will not usually be based on the fact that provision, for which a statement is not required may;

• have been tried and failed; or
• be inappropriate;

The decision to make a statement is most often based on whether a child is to have extra teaching or non-teaching help in his or her present school or is to be moved to a special school or unit which is classified as special educational provision.

A lack of defined special educational arrangements for children with the wider range of special educational needs often leads to premature pressure to institute the Act's assessment procedures for deciding whether to make a statement. A lack of clear terms of reference for what a child may receive from peripatetic and supporting services may lead to similar premature pressure. By matching a child's needs to the dimensions and levels of provision made by primary and secondary schools and support services the points at which the Act's assessment procedures, leading to the possibility of a statement, might be instituted, may become clearer.

The suggested framework of dimensions and levels can first of all be used as a check list of the variety of a child's needs. Have all the parameters of assessment been covered? Second, the appropriate level of intervention for that child on each dimension can be identified. This is a process to which assessment reports would be expected to contribute in their recommendations. A profile of a child's needs in terms of levels on each dimension might be drawn (Figure 9.1). Finally the decision whether to make a statement, or not, could be based on the authority's levels of provision for which this is considered necessary.

It would be necessary for local education authorities, working with health and social services, to develop an agreed set of levels of intervention for these services together with criteria for them. All professionals involved in assessment procedures would need to contribute to this development and to agree to the use of common criteria. This process should lead to descriptions of what children need that are more readily understood by all concerned.

Figure 9.1 illustrates the kind of profile that might be developed for an individual with a hearing loss receiving special education within a primary or secondary school. A profile of a similar kind might be developed for a particular form of provision, the tasks of a teacher and a training course.

It should be possible to match a profile against the profiles of different services and facilities available in the locality and the actions being taken, or likely to be taken, by health and social services. In practice, it will not always be possible to make a satisfactory match but the knowledge gained over time from gaps between levels of need and provision should lead to the more constructive planning and development of facilities and services.

The Characteristics of Provision

At present many needs are matched to hopes and good intentions rather than reality. Primary and secondary schools seldom describe their special educational arrangements in any detail. Support services and off-site facilities attempt to meet the aggregate of the needs of all the children referred to them rather than specifying which they can meet effectively with available resources. Special school staffs, in particular, describe what they provide in very general terms and often set their own terms of reference for admissions, modifying them according to the demand for places. Education authorities have not had a framework within which to develop special educational provision and have ended up with an accretion of elements, each often specifying their own functions, which are managed and developed in isolation one from another.

One current anomaly needs to be resolved. This concerns provision which Department of Education and Science guidance, Circular 1/83,[1] suggests is outside the scope of statement procedures. Most of this is in units and centres outside schools which cater for reading difficulties or for disruptive behaviour. An individual may be placed in such provision without comprehensive assessment and certainly without the parents having the rights which exist when a statement is made. It would be helpful if these kinds of provision were included in the grid of dimensions and levels even when a statement is not required for admission to them. They would:

- bring meeting the needs of children, who, attend them, within a coherent special education service; and
- give such provision an appropriate status since the level of needs and the work required to meet them may, in many cases, justify a statement.

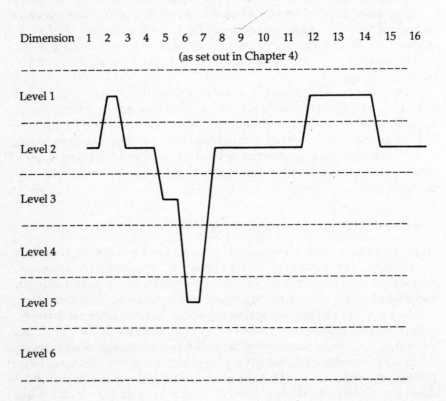

Figure 9.1

If we look back to the examples of available special education teacher time in primary and secondary schools (Chapter 3) we can now ask three questions.

- What is the nature and level of provision which might reasonably be expected in those schools given the resources available?
- What dimensions and levels of provision are expected to be made by the authority in the units it has set up in the schools?
- What dimensions and levels of need are likely to be met by the support services to the schools provided by the authority?

A framework of the kind outlined could provide a means of defining the responsibilities of all the elements of a comprehensive and integrated special educational service. Using such a framework an authority could begin to plan the coordinated development of provision which should follow a pattern of working from minimum to maximum intervention.

The first step would be to look at the resources that it is possible to assign to all primary and secondary schools, within local financial management, to meet the wider range of special educational needs. Having decided what is possible in general terms it will be necessary to make operational decisions about the dimensions and levels of provision it is reasonable to expect schools to make. This in itself will be insufficient without a mechanism to see that the assigned resources are used for the purpose.

A second step would be to look at the peripatetic and advisory support teaching services it is possible to provide to increase schools' capacities to help more children with special educational needs. The dimensions and levels of the work of these services will need to be defined.

Third, the authority will need to determine what kinds of unit it will provide within primary and secondary schools for what levels of special educational need. Because the units are provided by the authority, and therefore for children who are the subject of a statement, criteria for entry may automatically be related to the points at which statements of needs are made.

These first three steps may be relatively straightforward in present circumstances. The effect of new legislation will be to make them much more difficult. A coherent pattern of special educational provision may be increasingly difficult to develop with the fragmentation of the secondary school system. The delegation of financial management will lead to a very varied pattern of decision making, with market forces unlikely to respect minority interests or special needs.

The contribution of special schools, and units outside primary and secondary schools, provided by the authority, has often been determined by headteachers and teachers in charge. It is necessary for local education authorities to be much more active in negotiating the terms of reference of such schools and units with governors, headteachers and teachers. This should be facilitated by the suggested framework. Where its arrangements are inadequate the authority may need to seek provision elsewhere in non-maintained and independent special schools.

The proposed framework should enable authorities to describe and define the expected contributions of each of the elements within their special educational service. It would have particular relevance to the nature of arrangements the authority might expect to be made in its primary and secondary schools. It should help a general understanding of the nature and levels of the interventions that different support teaching services can make. Finally, it should help to define the contributions to be expected from special schools and units of all kinds.

In summary, the framework of dimensions and levels could provide a method of describing what is done, at what depth, in different forms of special education. This is something which does not exist at present.

Special Educational Job Descriptions

Special education teachers have a reputation for responding generously to need. Their willingness to take on extra work is well known. Many, especially those working in primary and secondary schools, in supporting services and in isolated units, are under pressure because of a lack of understanding of their work and an inadequate system to describe it. Such teachers should have clearer terms of reference.

Within schools, members of staff with special education respon- sibilities seldom have their contribution either assured or defined. This is often because the dimensions and levels of provision expected in these schools have not been made clear. It is often advantageous for such teachers to contribute both to the regular teaching programme and to special educational arrangements, but it is necessary for both to be given equal priority. The latter should not always be at the mercy of staff absences. Thus the duties of individual teachers might be defined in terms of dimensions of curriculum, contact type, time intensity and environ- ment in relation to specific kinds of special educational need.

In peripatetic and support services the question of the priority given to changing the context in which needs arise and to work with children has already been mentioned. There are also service issues such as the time devoted to individuals and to groups. The proposed framework should help. Each of the dimensions such as curriculum, contact type, time intensity, knowledge and skills might be used to plan a teacher's work. For example, a teacher might be able to meet the needs of X children with level 1 needs and Y children with level 2 needs on the contact type dimension in the available time.

Special schools and units would require teachers working in them to have different levels of experience and training. The framework and the description of the school or unit would indicate the levels of contribution along the particular dimensions teachers would be required to make. Again, over time, there would be an improving match between teachers and the situations to which they can contribute most effectively. This match would be facilitated if training arrangements themselves also recognised the proposed framework.

Planning Special Educational Services

The planning of most special educational services has been *ad hoc*. Demands and special interest groups have distorted priorities. With the kind of framework proposed, modified for local conditions, it should be possible for authorities to come to decisions about a number of aspects of their special educational provision. The dimensions and levels of intervention expected in each kind of provision can be decided. These principal areas of provision are:

1. the extent and level of arrangements expected within primary and secondary schools within delegated resources;
2. the extent and levels of provision to be made by peripatetic and support teaching services;
3. the extent and levels of provision made in units, set up by the authority, within primary and secondary schools;
4. the extent and levels of provision to be made in special schools and off-site units by the authority; and
5. the extent and levels of need for which provision will be sought elsewhere than in the authority.

The framework of dimensions and levels could then lead to operational decisions. For example, it might be decided that level 1 and 2 provision would be made in all primary and secondary schools and level 3 and 4 provision in special education units set up by the authority within them. Level 3 and 4 arrangements might also be made in off-site units and level 5 and 6 provision in day and boarding special schools.

Having made decisions of the kind suggested it would then become easier to decide on the criteria which should operate when deciding whether to make a statement of special educational needs and provision. An authority might, for example, decide that statements would only be required for level 4, 5 and 6 provision.

The planning envisaged will enable the use of available resources to be monitored and enable them to be switched to areas of greatest need. The proportion of available resources allocated to each dimension and level should give a better indication of an education authority's priorities. At present the allocation of resources and the evaluation of their use within special education is crude and unsatisfactory.

Planning Special Education Teacher Training

Special education teachers are assiduous course attenders. There have always been many opportunities to attend short courses and conferences. The programme of long courses took longer to develop and more recently has seen many more part-time opportunities than full-time ones.

The introduction of grant-related in-service training arrangements (GRIST) has presented local education authorities with new responsibilities for the nature of professional training and career planning. The first response of authorities appears to have been to significantly reduce the number of full-time secondments for long courses. Responsibilities have not always been accepted and, in some cases, they appear to have been avoided by responding to immediate short-term needs or by simply expecting schools to use proportional allocations of funds. The latter procedure will increase as greater financial management is delegated to schools.

Because of a lack of a framework for professional development based on levels of training, levels of work and levels of experience, the previous arrangements were far from satisfactory. Short courses provided fragmentary experience which were not cumulative. Long courses often attempted to provide for all levels of training in one course. To try and cover the range of knowledge and skills from classroom competence to leadership, management and research capabilities within 40 to 50 weeks is an impossible task.

The priorities determined by the Department of Education and Science within education support grants for training have helped considerably to develop training for levels of special education work expected in primary and secondary schools. But these time-limited grants appear likely to reflect short-term rather than long-term concerns.

An agreement on a general framework of dimensions for special education and the recognition of levels of skill and intervention would help to define training opportunities of different kinds. A hierarchy of training opportunities would be made more effective if approved short courses could contribute modules towards qualifications. The principle of levels of training and levels of work for which a person is qualified applies in other professions and might, with profit, be considered in the field of special education.

It will be difficult to develop any coherence in overall training arrangements when major decisions are made in thousands of individual

CHAPTER 10

Prospects

Introduction

New legislation will be implemented in the 1990s and its impact on the education system over the next decade is far from certain. These changes in the nature of the education system will be taking place while special education is attempting to complete its transformation from a separate system, based on a medical model, to an integral element in the education service. While it is by no means certain that the simplistic aims which have influenced its enactment will be achieved, the new legislation is unlikely to help this transformation process. It may, indeed, encourage a return to an 'individual deficit' model of special educational needs which ignores the environmental influences in schools and elsewhere, which create special educational needs.

Since the Warnock Report and the 1981 Act considerable attention has been given to individual assessment and programme planning. Special schools have reviewed their curriculum and developed more precise objectives. The curriculum, rather than treatment, has become a central feature of special education. But the nature of special education has received little attention.

What is Special Education?

In spite of all that has been said and written there are no easy, or indeed agreed, answers to this question. To ask a group of people to answer the following questions with a straight 'Yes' or 'No' will illustrate some of the different perspectives:

- Is special education a variation of regular education?
- Is it a separate and different form of education?
- Is it a generally curative classroom climate?
- Is it a specific programme to remediate an individual learning difficulty?
- Is it a support system to maintain an individual in primary or secondary education?
- Is it a therapy?

In some senses it is all these things in different combinations. In practice many individuals pick one or two of the possibilities to exemplify their understanding.

What do Special Education Teachers Do?

Another approach might be to ask a second set of questions. These might be addressed to those both outside and inside the field and ask what is actually being done. Some of these questions might be:

- What are the activities of:
  - special education teachers in a primary or secondary schools?
  - special education teachers in peripatetic and support teaching services?
  - special education teachers in special schools and units?
- What does special education teaching in these situations have in common?
- In what ways is special education teaching in these situations different from regular teaching?

To set out the questions is easy and many more could be added. The point of asking them is not to seek final or unanimous answers. It is to suggest that a framework of dimensions and levels could provide a basis for answering them and enable specialists and non-specialists to communicate more effectively.

Disseminating the Conceptual Framework

There are many informed and uninformed opinions, both professional and lay, brought to bear on the needs of children with disabilities and difficulties and the ways they might be met. These include an undemanding charity for the 'poor handicapped children', from whom, by implication, it is cruel to expect too much, an insensitive disregard of individual differences and preoccupations with very specific needs. Expectations of special education vary according to the experience and perspective of individuals. The mixture of lay, non-specialist and specialist opinions is complex. It is little wonder that there is no general agreement about what special education is and how it should be provided.

Before attempting to summarise the case for such an agreement it may be helpful to look at the large number of different interests which influence special education policies and which may need to understand any approach to common definitions. The different perspectives to be found at the local authority level may be summarised in the following way:

1. Management
   non-specialist:
   - elected members;
   - non-specialist authority officers;
   - non-specialist inspectors and advisors;
   - governors of primary and secondary schools; and
   - heads of primary and secondary schools.
   specialist:
   - authority officers responsible for special education.
   - special education inspectors and advisors; and
   - heads of special schools and units.
2. Teaching
   non-specialist:
   - primary and secondary school teachers.
   specialist:
   - special education teachers; and
   - the child's own teacher.
3. 'Parents'
   non-specialist:
   - parents of children in primary and secondary schools; and
   - social and child care workers.
   specialist:
   - the child's own parents;
   - foster parents.
4. Other
   non-specialist:
   - educational associations;
   - teacher associations;
   - civic groups; and

specialist:
- voluntary disability organisations;
- parents of children with special educational needs; and
- specialist professional associations.

The list of interests and potential contributors is long and shows how easy it is for general and specific interests to conflict and how difficult effective communication can be. A more precise framework and language of special education, it is suggested, might help to develop a common understanding of shared concerns.

The Need for Structure

Although many local education authorities have reorganised their special education services, relatively little attention has been devoted to the nature of special education systems within which to meet individually assessed needs.

The issue of what range of options should be or, in times of resource restraint, can be made available has not received serious attention. The relatively *ad hoc* accretion of facilities and services has rarely been subject to rational analysis. All too often sensitive assessment is followed by crude choices within a traditional pattern of provision.

One example may illustrate the need for more attention to the structures of service delivery. Since the 1981 Act many education authorities have been supporting an increasing number of children, who are the subject of statements, in regular classes. Support usually takes the form of additional teaching or non-teaching sessions. Each placement has often been dealt with separately. Large resource commitments have been made, without a policy framework, as a result of a response to individual cases.

The kind of teachers and assistants who have been used to give these extra sessions are usually neither experienced nor trained in special education. Is special education simply anything extra or anybody's time? Should it not be specified in terms of knowledge and experience and other dimensions?

A special education service, within which to fit supporting arrangements of this kind, has seldom been apparent. Schools have been uncertain about the support they will get or how they should use the additional time. Additional time has implicitly been equated with special education. Without an agreed structure, attempting to meet individual needs, and giving more choice, may lead to chaotic competition for limited resources.

What kinds of service-delivery system do we need to be able to respond flexibly to individual needs, individual parental choices and teacher concerns? This book has been arguing for a conceptual framework on which to base the practical implementation of a comprehensive service delivery system. It has suggested that the question 'What is special education?' has not received sufficient attention and that there are few agreed answers to it. A framework of the kind suggested may not be the answer; but if it is not what alternatives are there?

The model assumes that all forms of special education are part of a single delivery service working towards the same objectives: increasing the efficiency of primary and secondary education in responding to individual differences. It has defined characteristics or dimensions of special education and suggested that there should be a series of levels of intervention along each dimension. Such a structure should make it easier to describe the nature of a particular form of special education and specify what is being provided for individuals.

A Basis for Defining Special Education

At present there is only a crude and general language to describe special education. Its location, the qualifications of teachers and the grouping of children are often the only agreed characteristics. It is necessary to develop a more detailed descriptive system within a changing pattern of education. This descriptive system should take into account resource management and planning. The current language used to describe special education is not adequate for this purpose.

The 1981 Act definitions of special educational need and provision are relative to learning abilities and to educational provision in an area. What is being suggested is an extension of that relativity to specific characteristics of education in regular classes.

It is argued that the operational basis for defining special education must be the degree of variation in essential characteristics or dimensions of primary and secondary education. For a child with special educational needs, provision should be defined by the level of variation or intervention necessary on those dimensions. For service-delivery systems the framework of dimensions and levels should define more precisely what different elements in a special education service are providing and what is contributed by different professionals.

Relativity is a Positive Advantage

Although relativity creates difficulties for administrators and professionals it is a positive approach. It assumes a continued improvement in the capacity of primary and secondary schools to deal appropriately with individual differences. It assumes a decreasing need for special educational arrangements in primary and secondary schools and

elsewhere as this capacity increases. It also assumes that all elements in a
special education system, including special schools, are directing their
efforts to the same ends: improving this capacity in those schools.

These assumptions are essential for the health of the education system
as a whole. The principal alternatives involve;

- a decrease in the flexibility of schools to respond to individual
  differences;
- a continuing increase in the numbers of children with difficulties and
  disorders of all kinds which primary and secondary schools reject or
  are not expected to educate; and
- an increase in costly, separate, specialist facilities.

Concluding Summary

The previous chapters have attempted to give one answer to the
following questions:

- What are the characteristics or dimensions of good average regular
  education which may need to be varied?
- What might be appropriate degrees of variation on a dimension which
  could be developed as practical levels of intervention for professionals and services?
- What are the resource implications of different levels of intervention
  on each dimension?
- What levels of intervention, along which dimensions, are appropriate
  in different forms of service and provision?

Answers to these questions, which are appropriate to the time and to
the locality, will be an important step in maintaining special education
within the mainstream of educational thinking. To fail to answer them
may result in a return to a charitable, low demand, cosy system of special
education for individuals seen to have little to contribute to society.

The accountability for children's progress and standards now being
introduced into primary and secondary education will or should be
applied to special education. Children with special educational needs do
not require exemption from national standards. Like all other children
they require appropriate standards or targets.

At present the assessed needs of children cannot easily be transmuted
into the appropriate levels of skill, curriculum, technology and environmental modification required to meet them. Administrators and
professionals need criteria for allocating additional or different resources
of all kinds. At present they have only labelled children. It is argued that
it will be helpful to have national agreement about the major dimensions

necessary to describe acceptable special educational arrangements and thus the general level of resourcing required. There will, as at present, be local variation in levels of intervention as a result of education authority policies, priorities and resources.

The contributions of special education to a more fragmented school system, in which school-based management and resource decisions will be made, will be increasingly difficult to specify without an appropriate descriptive system. At local level at least there should be agreed parameters for the nature and degree of different levels of intervention. These will need to be defined in resource terms which include teacher skill, teacher time, environmental modification and technology.

The purpose of this book has been to initiate discussion of the question 'What is special education?' Having asked the question it is necessary to attempt to answer it. It is hoped that the answer given will be accepted as provisional and as a basis for discussion. It would be unhelpful if the suggested framework were to be seen as a straitjacket. The current complex pattern of special educational facilities and services urgently needs a rationale for planning which improves communication and harnesses the considerable efforts of those who work in the field towards common ends.

Index